AF255599

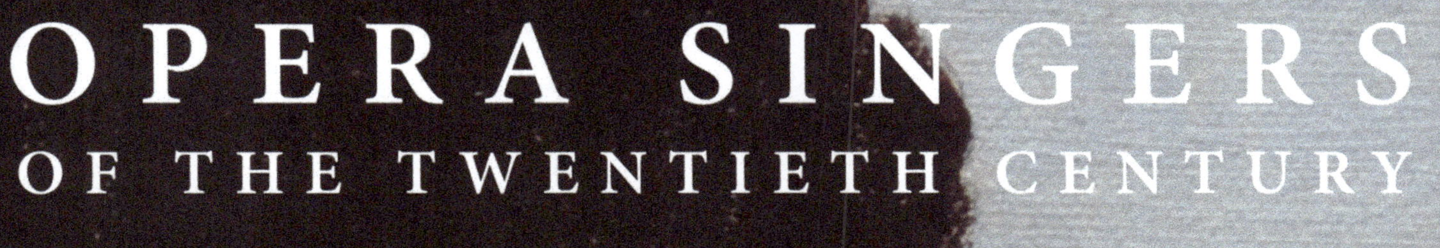

OPERA SINGERS
OF THE TWENTIETH CENTURY

SELECTED PORTRAITS and BIOGRAPHIES

Thomas Crawford

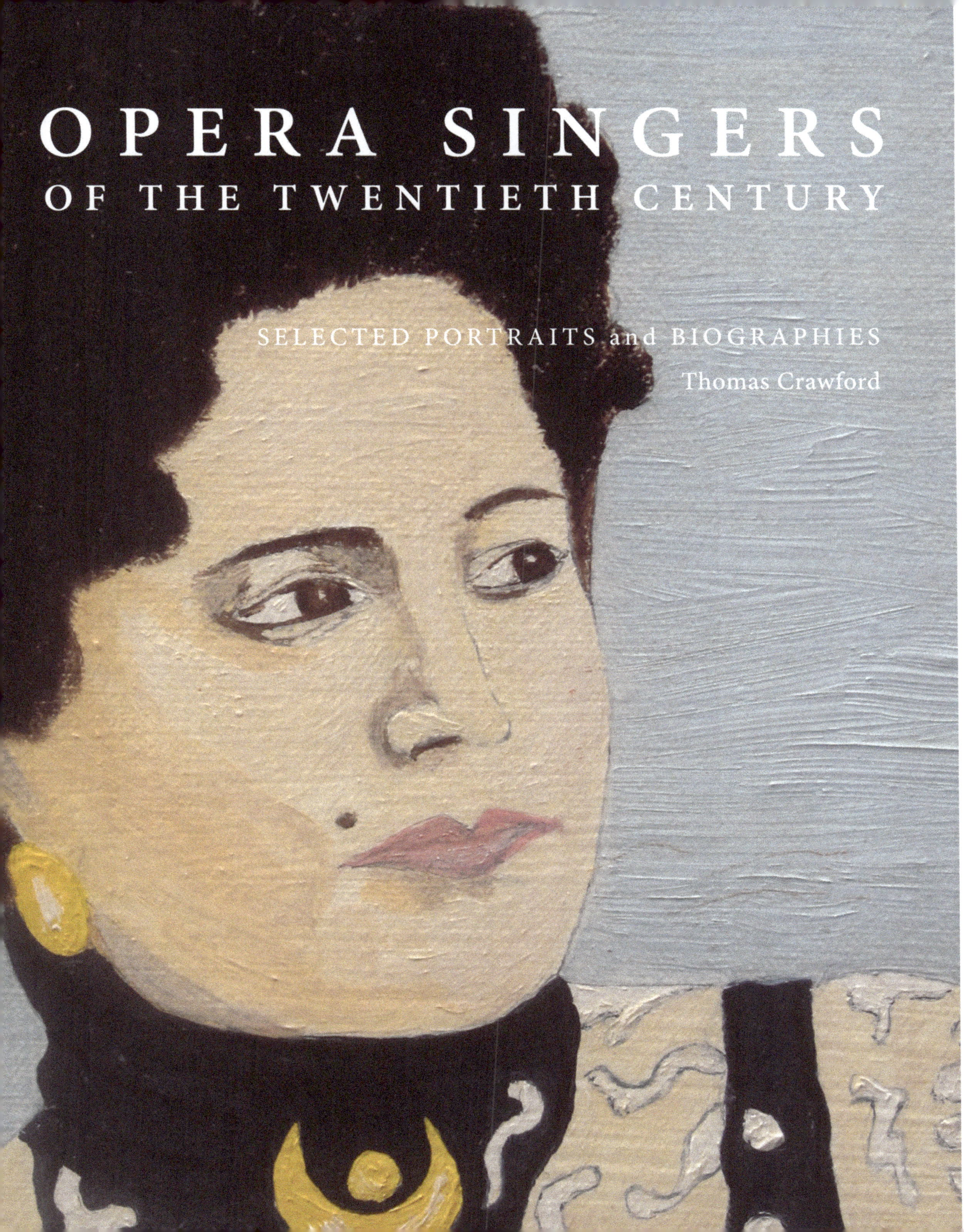

WORKBOOK PRESS LLC
187 E Warm Springs Rd,
Suite B285, Las Vegas, NV 89119, USA

Website: https://workbookpress.com/
Hotline: 1-888-818-4856
Email: admin@workbookpress.com

Ordering Information:
Quantity sales. Special discounts are available on quantity purchases by corporations, associations, and others.
For details, contact the publisher at the address above.

ISBN-13:   978-1-954753-04-4 (Paperback Version)
                  978-1-954753-02-0 (Digital Version)

REV. DATE: 29/06/2022

OPERA SINGERS
OF THE TWENTIETH CENTURY

SELECTED PORTRAITS AND BIOGRAPHIES

by Thomas Crawford

DEDICATION

Thomas Crawford's interest in opera and painting developed during his childhood in Burbank, California. He is a graduate of Stanford University and George Washington University Law School, was in the U.S. Navy and U.S. Foreign Service, and practiced law in San Francisco.

Essentially self-taught, his paintings have been exhibited at the Carole Cleaver Rodman Gallery in Oakland, New Jersey, the Ward-Nasse Gallery in New York City, and the George Krevsky Gallery in San Francisco. His work is in the permanent collection of the Negro Leagues Baseball Museum in Kansas City, Missouri.

He dedicates this book to his wife Caroline Cooley Crawford, formerly with the San Francisco Opera and presently a music historian at the Bancroft Library, University of California, Berkeley, and to two inspiring, brilliant artists, Tita Cooley Palmieri and Martha Crawford.

 Long live the recorded voices of opera singers around the world.

INTRODUCTION

The oil painting portraits collected in this book present some of the most eminent opera singers of the twentieth century. It is not a definitive list because no such list is possible. Most opera lovers would probably include these particular artists in any great performers list and would most likely place Caruso, Chaliapin, Bjoerling, Callas, Tebaldi, Flagstad, Melchior, Pinza and Pavarotti near the top. Most aficionados would also have a dozen other singers, not portrayed here, in their own selection of eminent singers.

The world of opera is so rich in international talent that any compilation by a mere enthusiast must necessarily be abitrary, incomplete, and reflect personal taste and one's experience with live performances and recordings.

The singers are depicted in some of their best-known roles and their careers described in brief biographies. The composers of the operas represented by the singers are also described in brief accompanying biographies.

Thomas Crawford

LIST OF SINGERS

MARIAN ANDERSON
Contralto

Born in Philadelphia, Pennsylvania, 1902; died in Portland, Oregon, 1993. Debut: in a London recital in 1930. Formal New York debut, 1935, at Town Hall. Her big, velvety voice was ideally suited to many operatic roles but such assignments were denied to her because of race. Known primarily for her performances of oratorio, lieder and spirituals, late in her career she became the first black soloist to appear at the Met, singing five performances of Ulrica (*Un ballo in maschera*) in 1955.

Marian Anderson as Ulrica
(*Un ballo in maschera*)

Un ballo in maschera, opera in 3 acts by **Giuseppe Verdi**, First performed in Rome, Teatro Apollo, 1859.

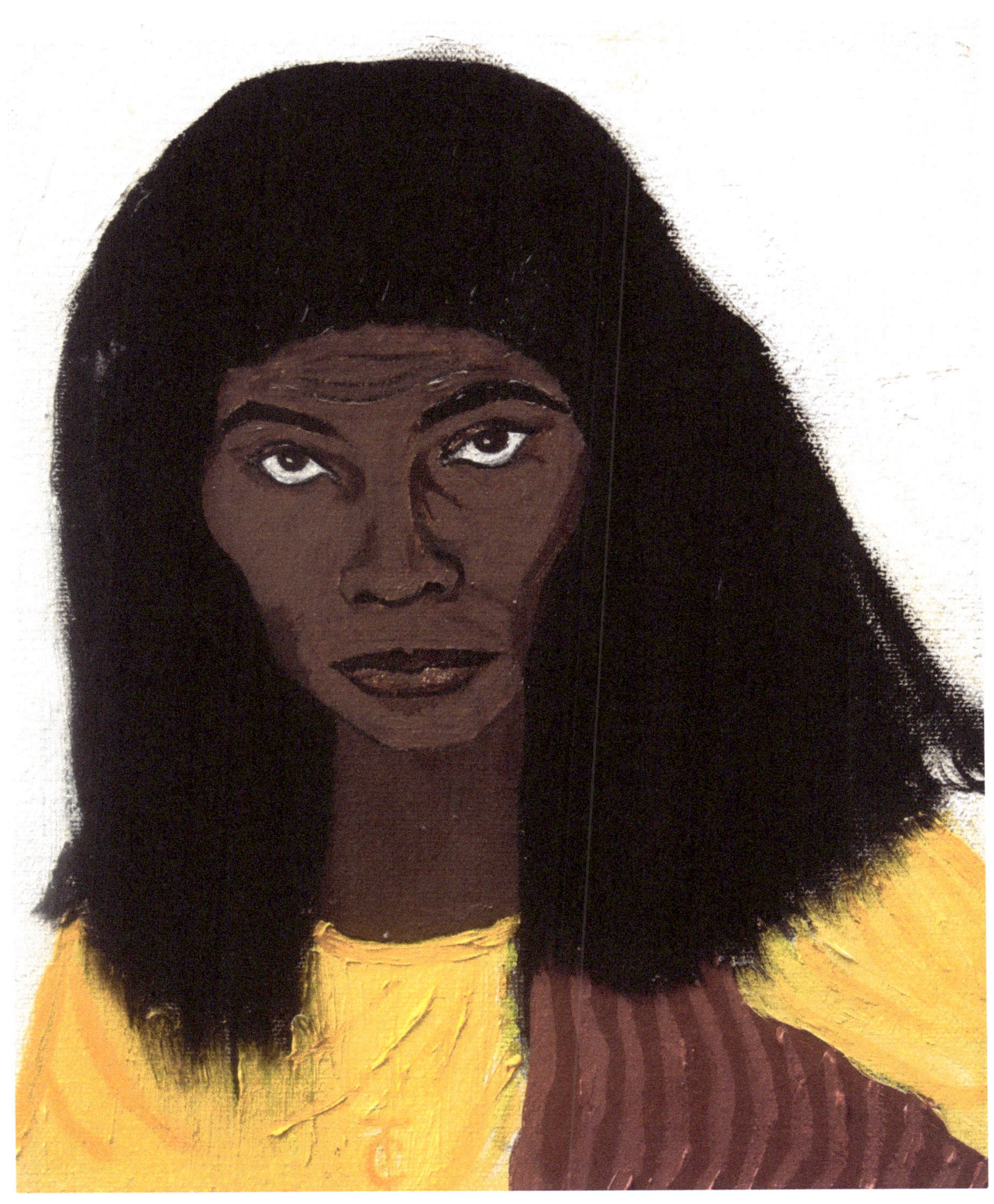

JUSSI BJOERLING
Tenor

Born in Stora Tuna, Sweden, 1911; died in Stockholm, Sweden, 1960. Debuts: Royal Opera, Stockholm, 1930, as Ottavio (*Don Giovanni*); Vienna, 1936; Chicago, 1937, as the Duke (*Rigoletto*); the Met, 1938, as Rodolfo (*La Bohème*). In the Italian repertoire, in which he specialized, Bjoerling was the outstanding singer of the mid-twentieth century.

Jussi Bjoerling as Riccardo
(*Un ballo in maschera*)

Un ballo in maschera, opera in 3 acts by **Giuseppe Verdi**, first performed in Rome, Teatro Apollo, 1859.

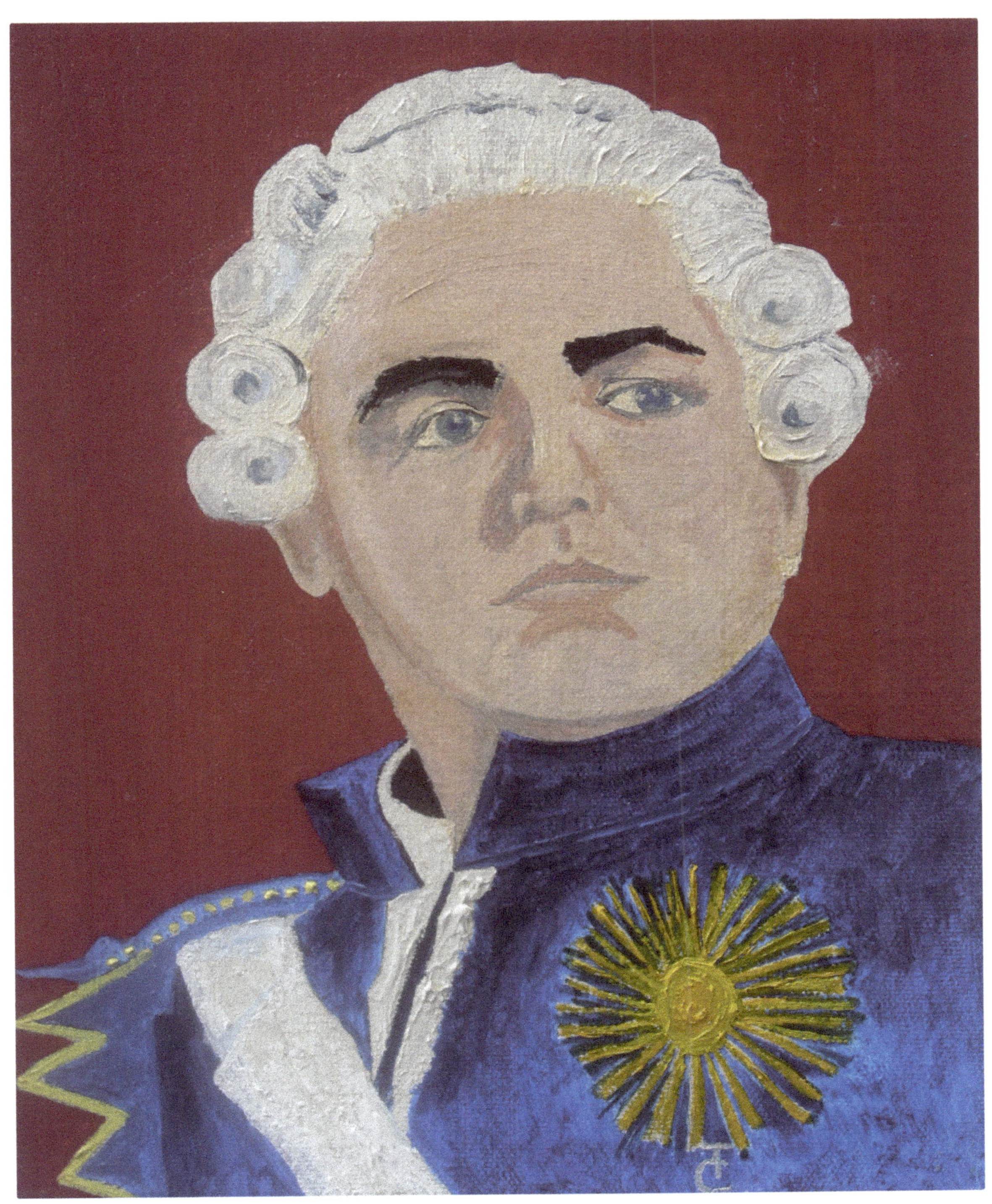

MARIA CALLAS
Soprano

Born in New York, N.Y., 1923; died in Paris, France, 1977.
She studied at the Athens Conservatory and made her
professional debut as Beatrice (*Boccaccio*) at the Royal Opera
in Athens in 1941. Her Italian debuts were as Gioconda at the
Verona Arena in 1947 and as Aida at La Scala in 1950. Norma was
her debut role at Covent Garden (1952), Chicago (1954) and the
Met (1956). Under the direction of Serafin and Visconti she
became the outstanding operatic actress of her time.

Maria Callas as Floria Tosca
(*Tosca*)

Tosca, opera in 3 acts by **Giacomo Puccini**,
first performed in Rome, Teatro Costanzi, 1900.

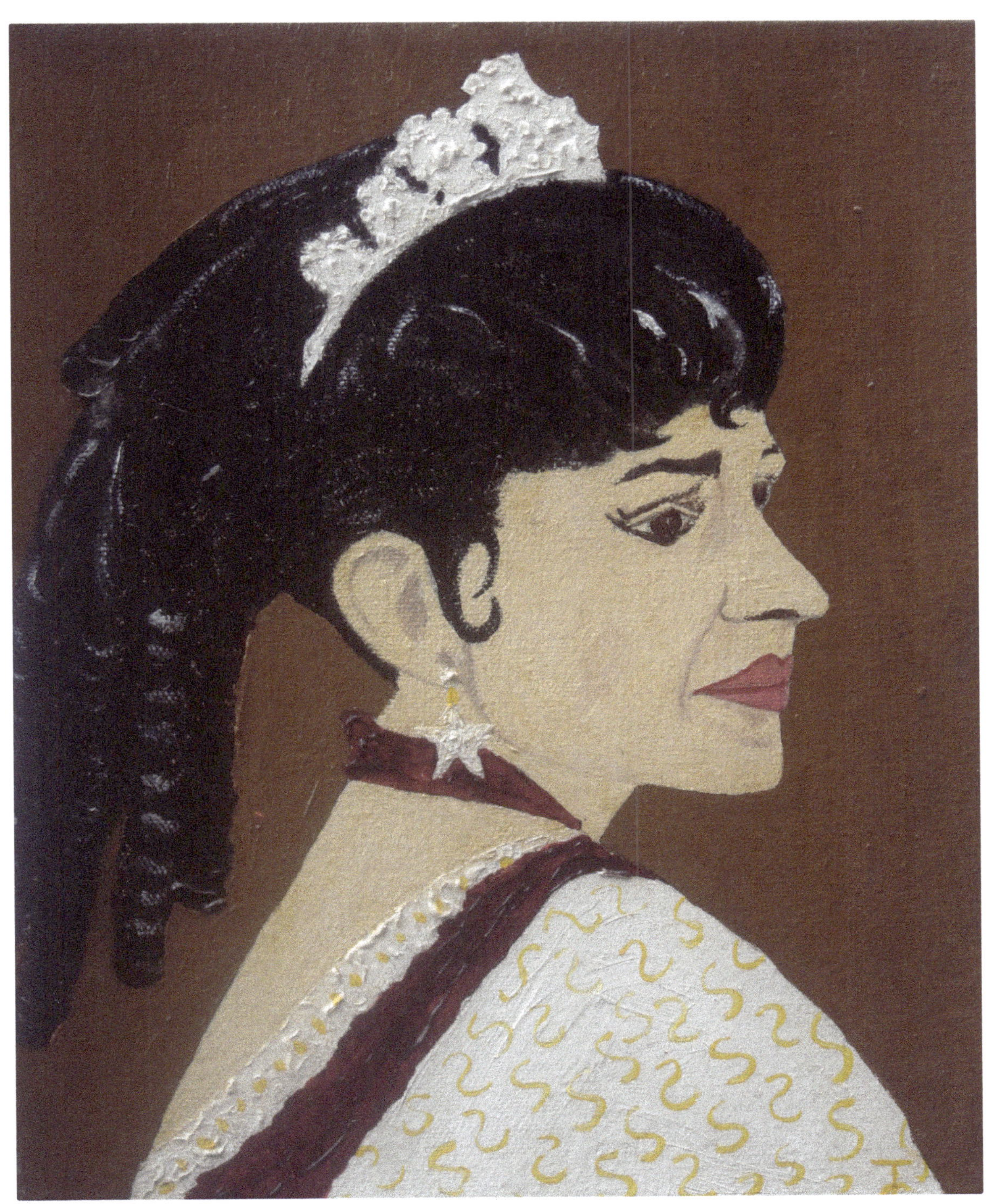

EMMA CALVÉ
Mezzo

Born in Decazeville, France, 1858; died in Millau, France, 1942. Debuts: Brussels, 1881, as Marguerite (*Faust*); La Scala, 1887; the Met, 1893, as Santuzza. Massenet wrote the mezzo leads in *La Navarraise* (1894) and *Sappho* (1897) for Calvé. She was most renowned for her legendary, earthy interpretation of Carmen, a role she sang at the Met 61 times, the first in 1893.

Emma Calvé as Carmen
(*Carmen*)

Carmen, opera in 4 acts by **Georges Bizet**,
first performed in Paris, Opera-Comique, 1875.

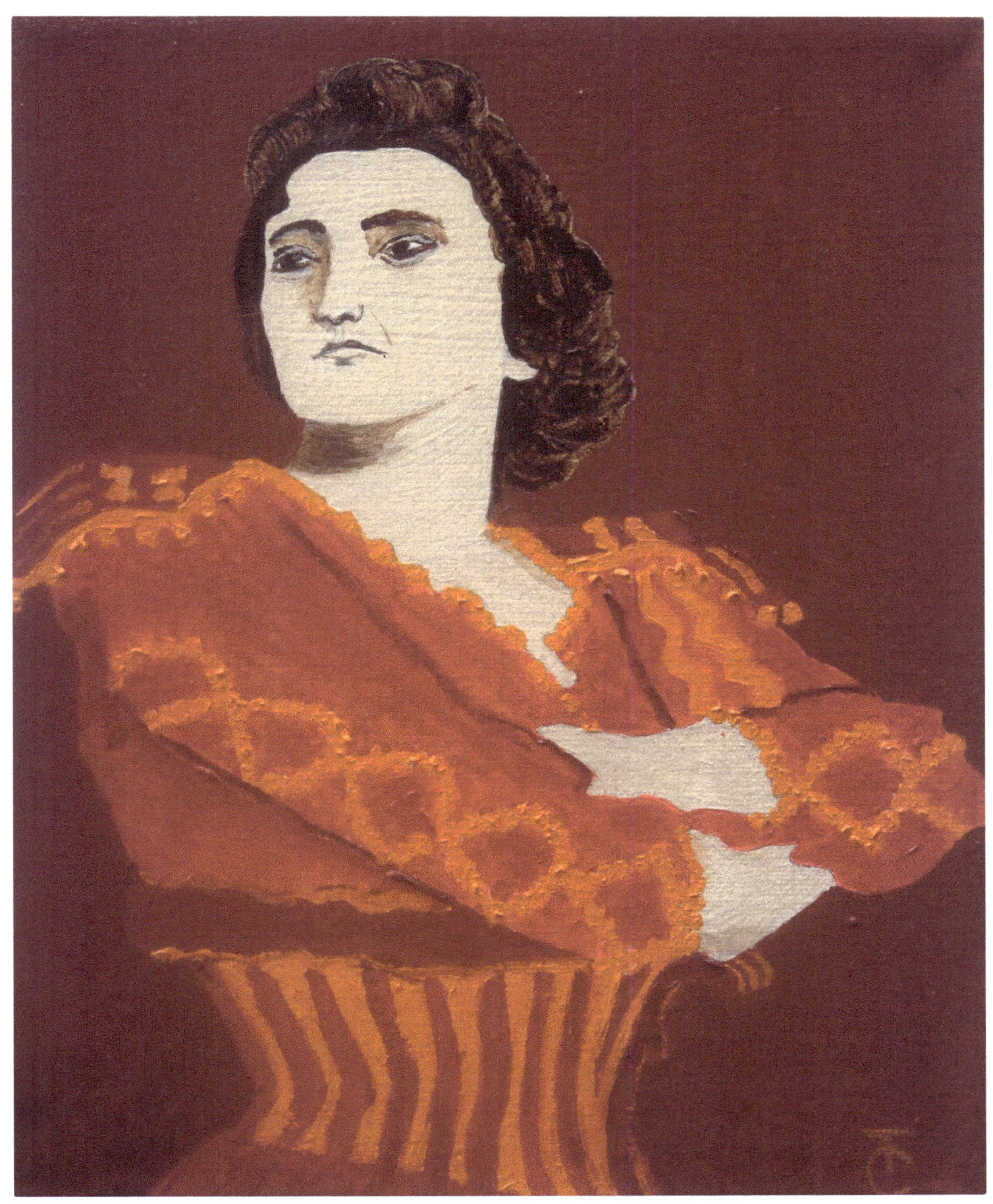

ENRICO CARUSO
Tenor

Born in Naples, Italy, 1873; died in Naples, Italy, 1921.
His debut in Naples, 1894, in Morelli's *L'amico Francesco*, led
to engagements all over Italy, including La Scala, 1900, when he
first appeared as Nemorino. He made his debut at Covent Garden
in 1902; and as the Duke (*Rigoletto*) in 1903 at the Met, where he
sang for 18 seasons. He created the tenor roles in *Fedora*, *Adriana
Lecouvreur*, *Germania*, and *La Fanciulla del West*. He built a repertory
of approximately 50 roles, both lyric and dramatic. A great recording
artist, he was the archtypal tenor of the 20th century and probably
the most famous singer of all time.

Enrico Caruso as Nemorino
(L'Elisir d'Amore)

L'Elisir d'Amore, opera comica in 2 acts by **Gaetano Donizetti**,
first performed in Milan, Teatro della Cannobiana, 1832.

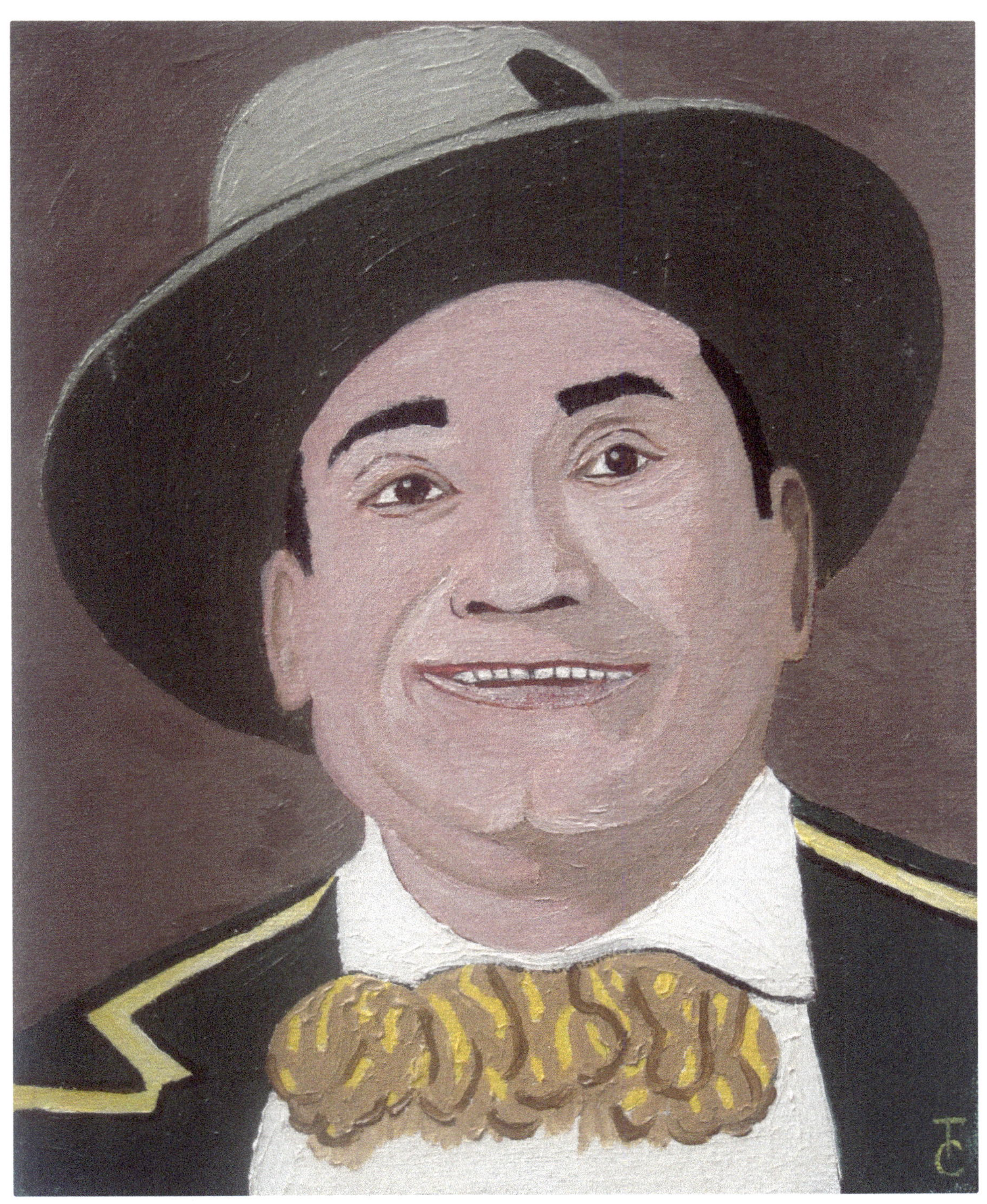

FEODOR IVANOVICH CHALIAPIN
Bass

Born in Kazan, Russia, 1873; died in Paris, France, 1938.

Debuts: Ufa, 1890; Tblisi, 1893; St. Petersburg, 1895; La Scala, 1901 as
Boito's Mephistopheles; the Met, 1908, as Mozart's Leporello (*Don Giovanni*).
Of peasant origin, Chaliapin had little formal education and was largely
self-taught. He studied briefly with his only teacher, Usatov, who taught
him for free. In 1893 he learned over 14 roles in five months. He built up
an extensive repertoire of Russian, French, and Italian operas. He is
recognized as one of the greatest recording artists
of the early 20th century.

Feodor Chaliapin as Boris
(*Boris Godunov*)

Boris Godunov, opera in prologue and 4 acts by **Modest Moussorgsky**,
first performed in St. Petersburg, Russia, 1874.

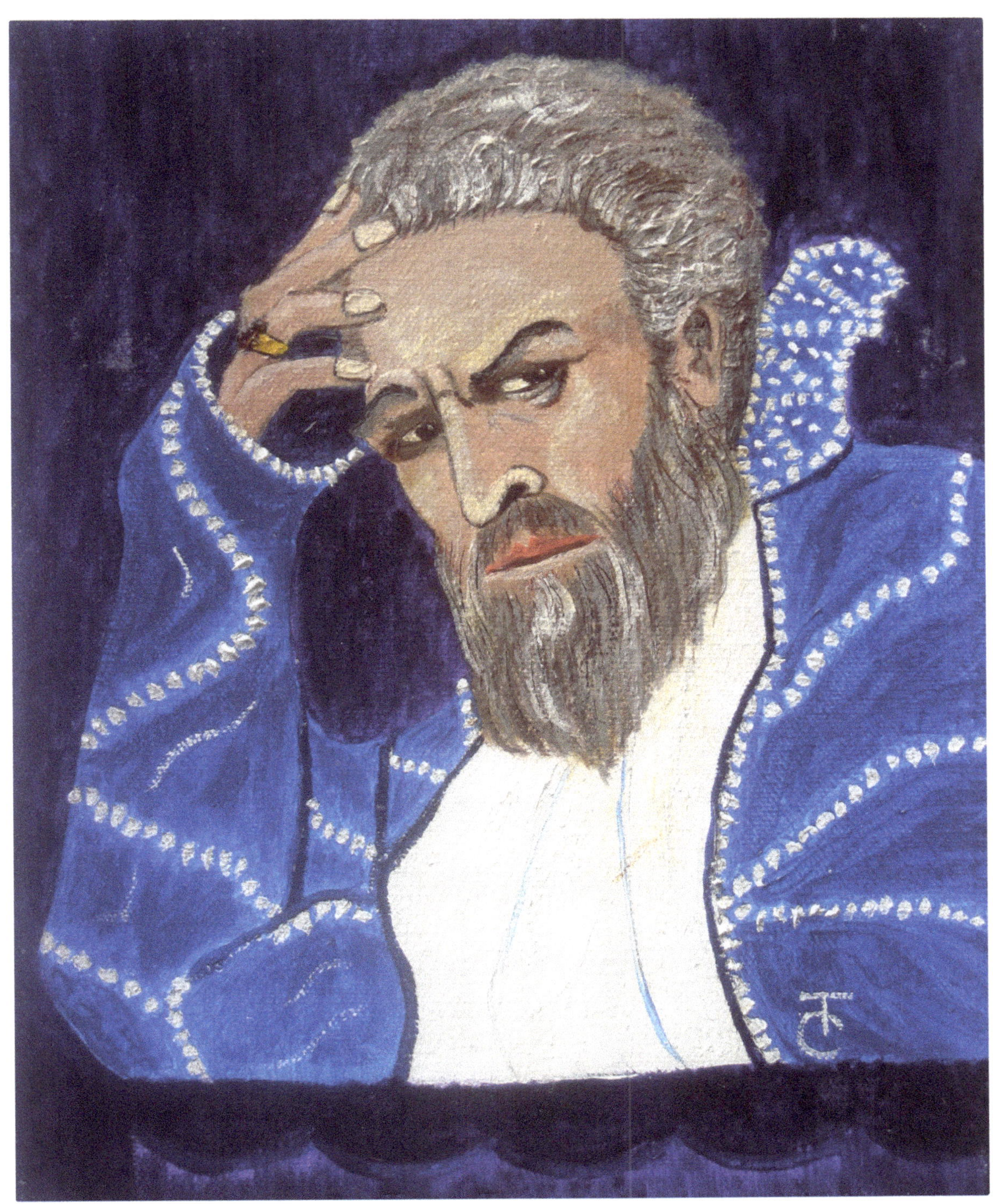

FRANCO CORELLI
Tenor

Born in Ancona, Italy, 1923, died in Milan, Italy, 2003.
Debuts: Spoleto, 1951, as Don José; La Scala, 1954, as Licinio in
La Vestale; Covent Garden, 1957, as Cavaradossi. He made his Met
debut in 1961 as Manrico and appeared each year thereafter, until
1974. Corelli had a wide international public following because his
fine spinto tenor voice was combined with leading-man appearance
and a commanding stage presence.

Franco Corelli as Don José
(*Carmen*)

Carmen, opera in 4 acts by **Georges Bizet**,
first performed at Paris Opera-Comique in 1875.

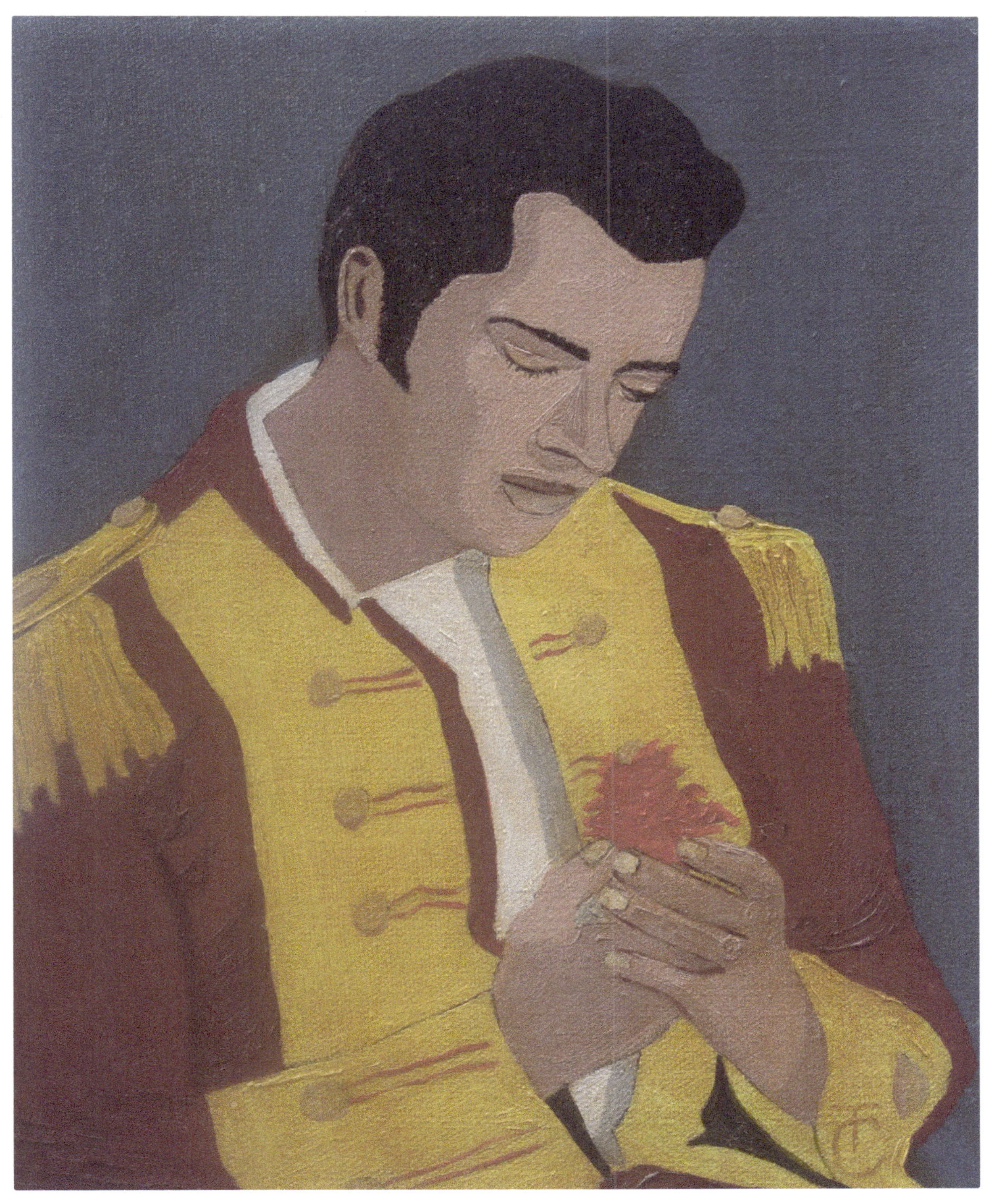

RÉGINE CRESPIN
Mezzo

Born in Marseille, France, 1927; died in Paris, France, 2007.
Debut: Mulhouse, 1950, as Elsa (*Lohengrin*), a role she repeated
for her Paris Opera debut, 1951. She created the role of the Nouvelle
Prieure in Poulenc's *Les Dialogues des Carmelites*, 1957. She sang
Kundry (*Parsifal*) at Bayreuth in 1958-60 and was an outstanding
Marschallin (*Der Rosenkavalier*) at Glyndebourne in 1959-60, her
debut role at Covent Garden (1960) and the Met (1962). Almost
uniquely in her time, she commanded the French dramatic repertoire.

Régine Crespin as Dido
(*Les Troyens*)

Les Troyens, opera in 5 acts by **Hector Berlioz**,
first performed in Paris, Théâtre Lyrique, in 1863.

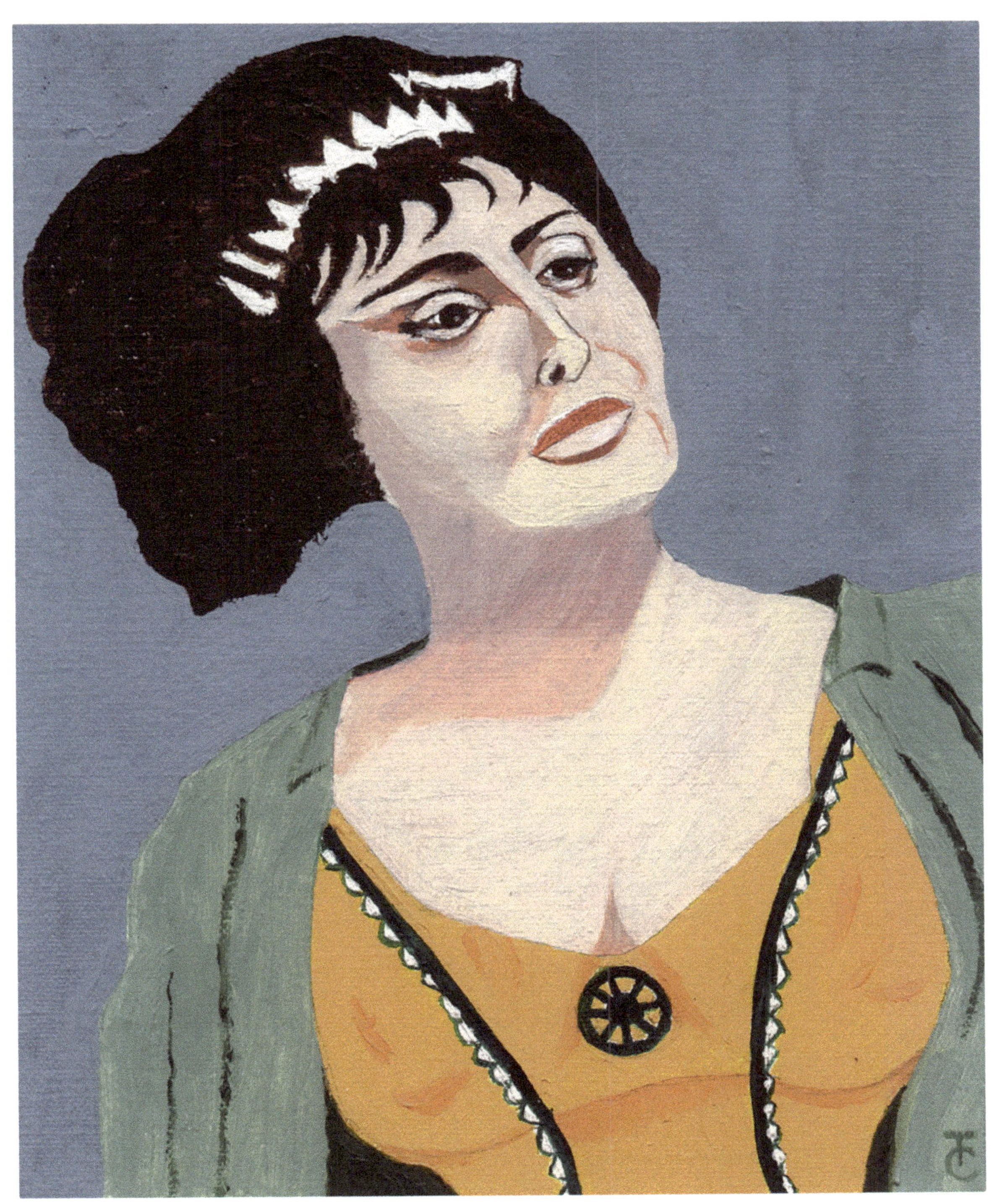

GIUSEPPE DE LUCA
Baritone

Born in Rome, Italy, in 1876; died in New York, N.Y., 1950.
Debuts: Piacenza, 1897, as Valentin (*Faust*). He created the principal
baritone roles of Michonnet in *Adriana Lecouvreur* (1902) and of
Sharpless in *Madama Butterfly* (1908) at La Scala. He starred at the
Teatro Colon, Buenos Aires, and sang in Barcelona, Vienna , Moscow
and St. Petersburg before making his Met debut as Figaro in 1915. He
remained the Verdi baritone at the Met for 20 years, forming
a legendary partnership with Giovanni Martinelli.

Giuseppe de Luca as Rigoletto

(*Rigoletto*)

Rigoletto, opera in 3 acts by **Giuseppe Verdi**,
first performed in Venice, La Fenice, 1851.

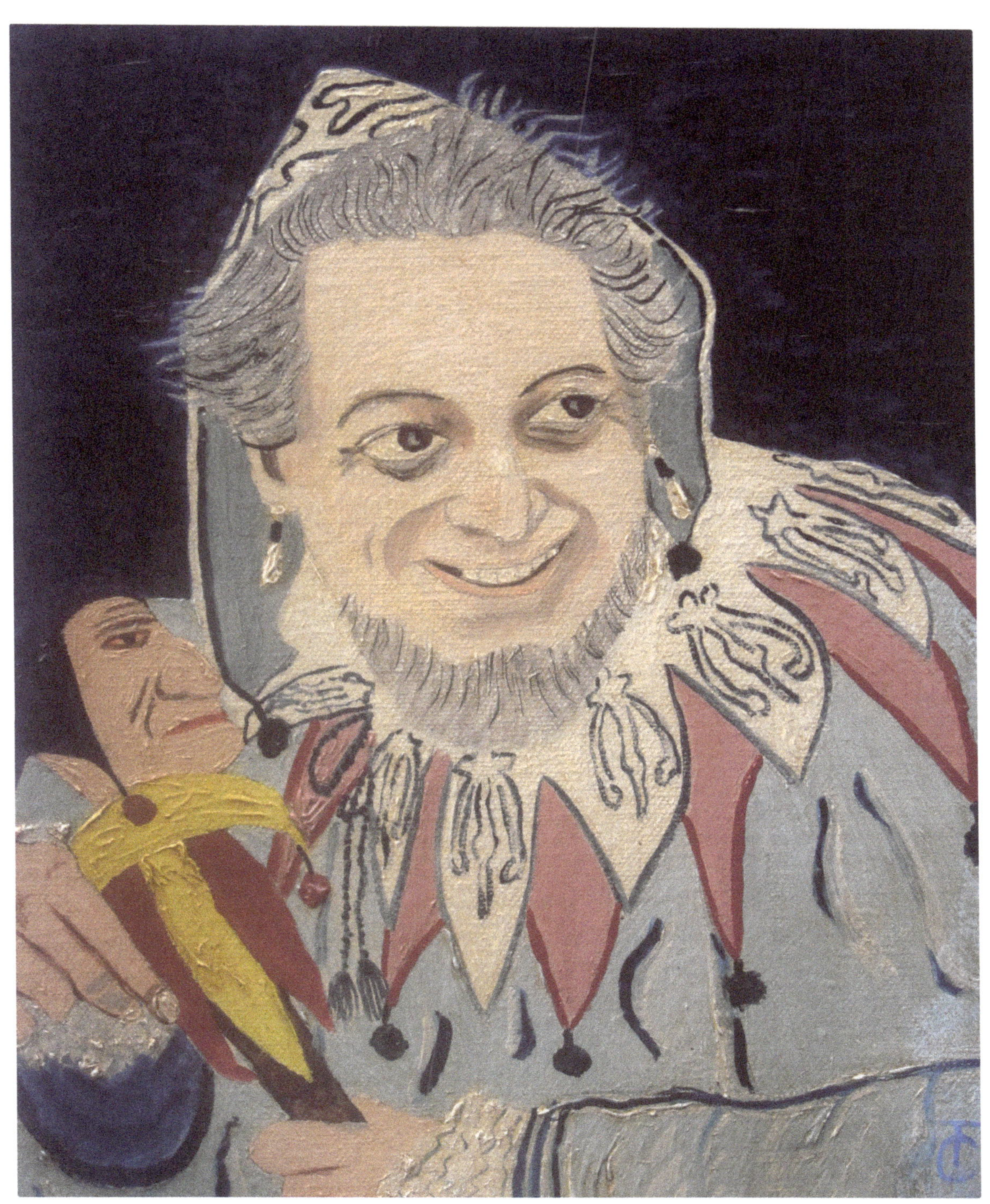

ÉDOUARD DE RESZKE
Bass

———◆———

Born in Warsaw, Poland, 1853; died in Garnek, Poland, 1917.
Debuts: Paris, 1876, as the King, in the first Paris production
of *Aida* with Verdi conducting; La Scala, 1879, creating Ruben
in Ponchielli's *Il Figliuol Prodigo*; Covent Garden, 1890, as Indra
(*Roi de Lahore*); Chicago, as Heinrich (*Lohengrin*) and New York
as Frère Laurent (*Romeo et Juliette*), both in 1891. He sang Wagner
first in Italian, then, after 1896, relearned the operas in German.
He and his brother Jean, tenor, are probably the
greatest sibling singers in opera.

Édouard de Reszke as Mephistopheles
(*Faust*)

Faust, opera in 5 acts by **Charles Gounod**,
first performed at Paris, Theatre-Lyrique, 1859.

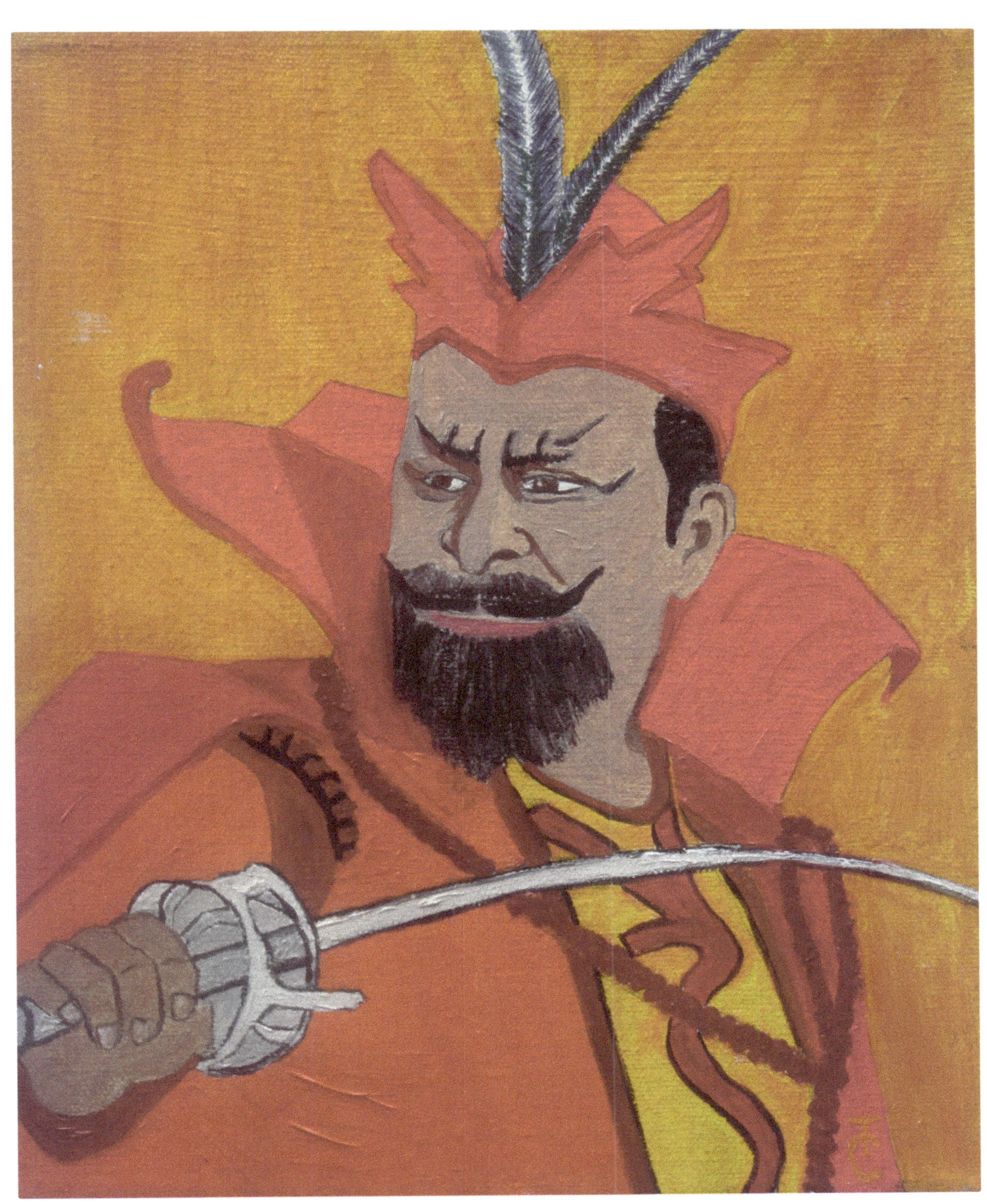

MARIO DEL MONACO
Tenor

Born in Florence, Italy, 1915; died in Venice, Italy, 1982.
Debuts: Milan Teatro Puccini, as Pinkerton (*Madama Butterfly*), 1941,
while on leave from the Italian army; 1945, Verona Arena, as Radames
(*Aida*); 1946, Covent Garden as Cavaradossi (*Tosca*); and 1950, San
Francisco as Radames, and the Met as Des Grieux (*Manon Lescaut*).
He was the most admired Otello of the mid-20th century, a role
which he performed 427 times and with which he was so
identified that he was buried in his Otello costume.

Mario del Monaco as Canio
(*I Pagliacci*)

I Pagliacci, opera in a prologue and 2 acts by **Ruggiero Leoncavallo**,
first performed Milan, Teatro dal Verme, 1892.

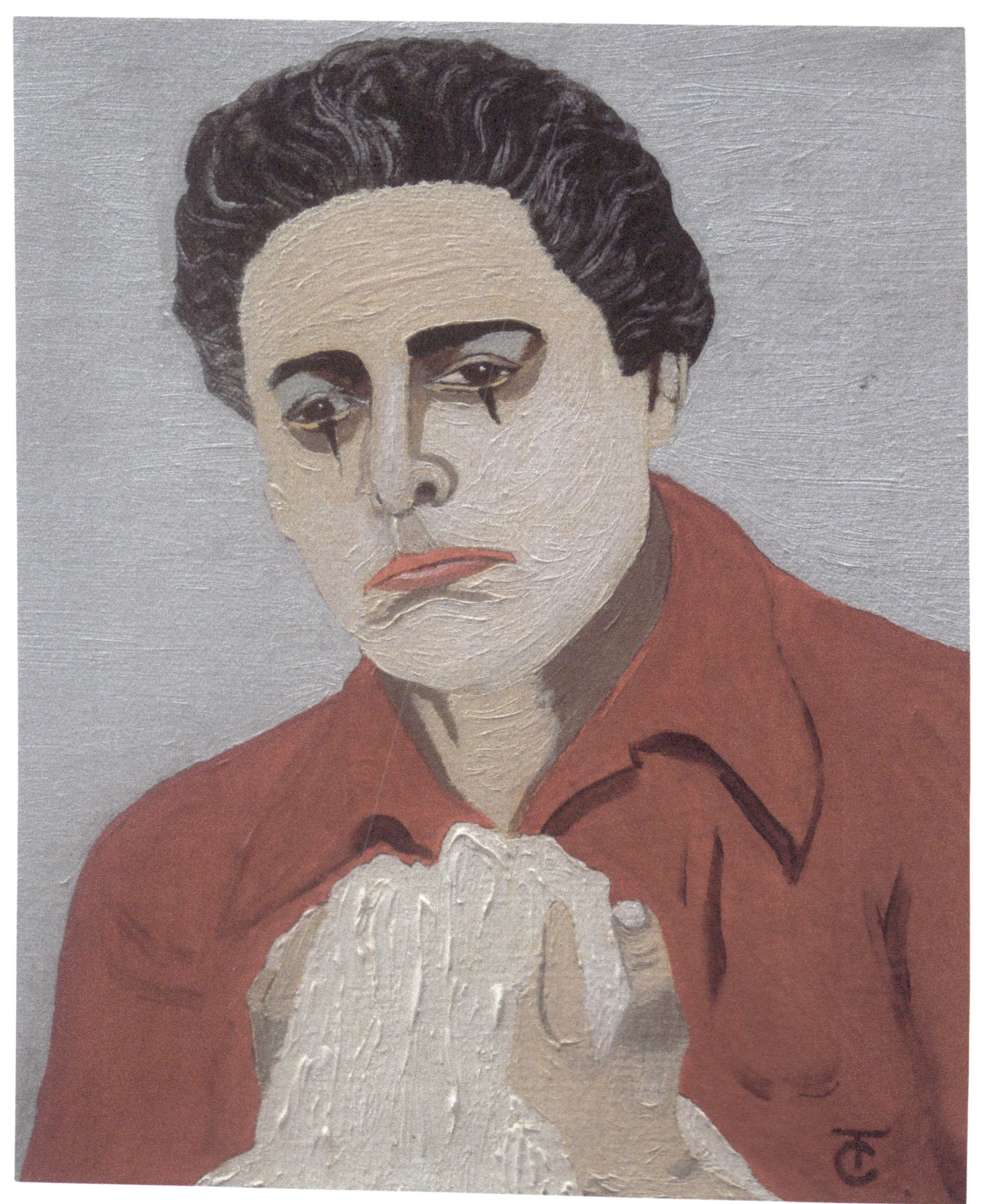

EMMY DESTINN
Soprano

Born in Prague, Czechoslavakia, 1878; died in Ceske Budejovice, Czechoslavakia, 1930. Debuts: Dresden (1897); Kroll Theater, Berlin, 1898, as Santuzza (*Cavalleria rusticana*); Bayreuth (1902) as Senta (*Der fliegende Hollaender*); and Covent Garden (1904) as Donna Anna (*Don Giovanni*). Richard Strauss selected her to sing Salome in Berlin and Paris. She made her Met debut in 1908 and sang there with Caruso in the premiere of *La Fanciulla del West* (1910).

Emmy Destinn as Marie
(*The Bartered Bride*)

The Bartered Bride, comic opera in 3 acts by **Bedrich Smetana**, first performed in Prague in 1866.

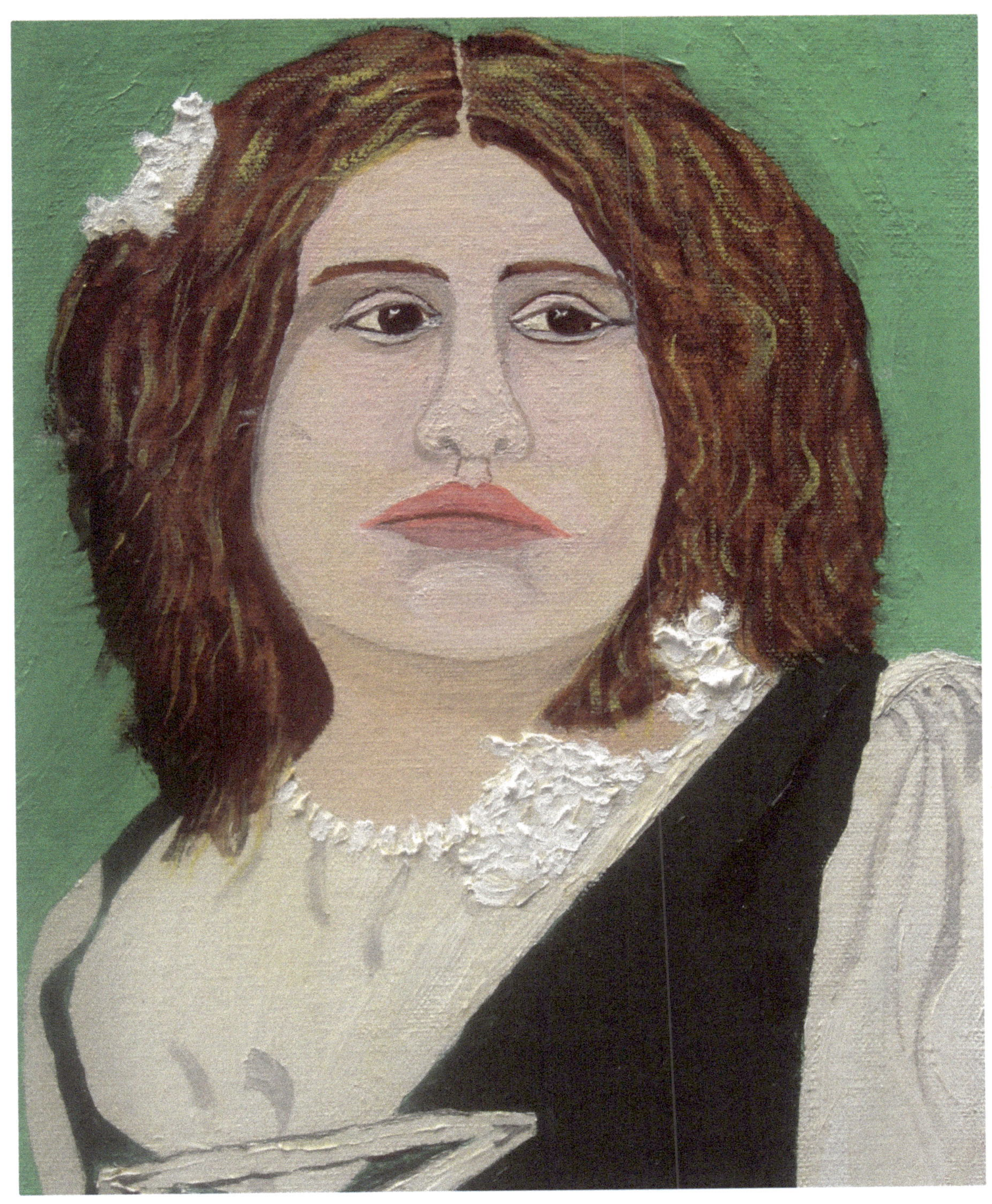

PLACIDO DOMINGO
Tenor

Born in Madrid, Spain, 1941. The son of Zarzuela performers, he was raised in Mexico City where he studied piano, conducting and singing. His first major role was Alfredo (*La Traviata*) in Mexico in 1960. From 1962 to 1965 he was a member of the Tel Aviv opera company. He debuted at the Met as Maurizio (*Adriana Lecouvreur*) in 1968, at La Scala in *Ernani,* 1969, and at Covent Garden in *Tosca,* 1971. He has probably sung more performances in more roles than any major tenor of the 20th century.

Placido Domingo as Hoffmann
(*Les Contes D'Hoffmann*)

Les Contes D'Hoffmann, a fantasy in 3 acts with a prologue and an epilogue by **Jacques Offenbach**, first performed in Paris, Opera-Comique, in 1881.

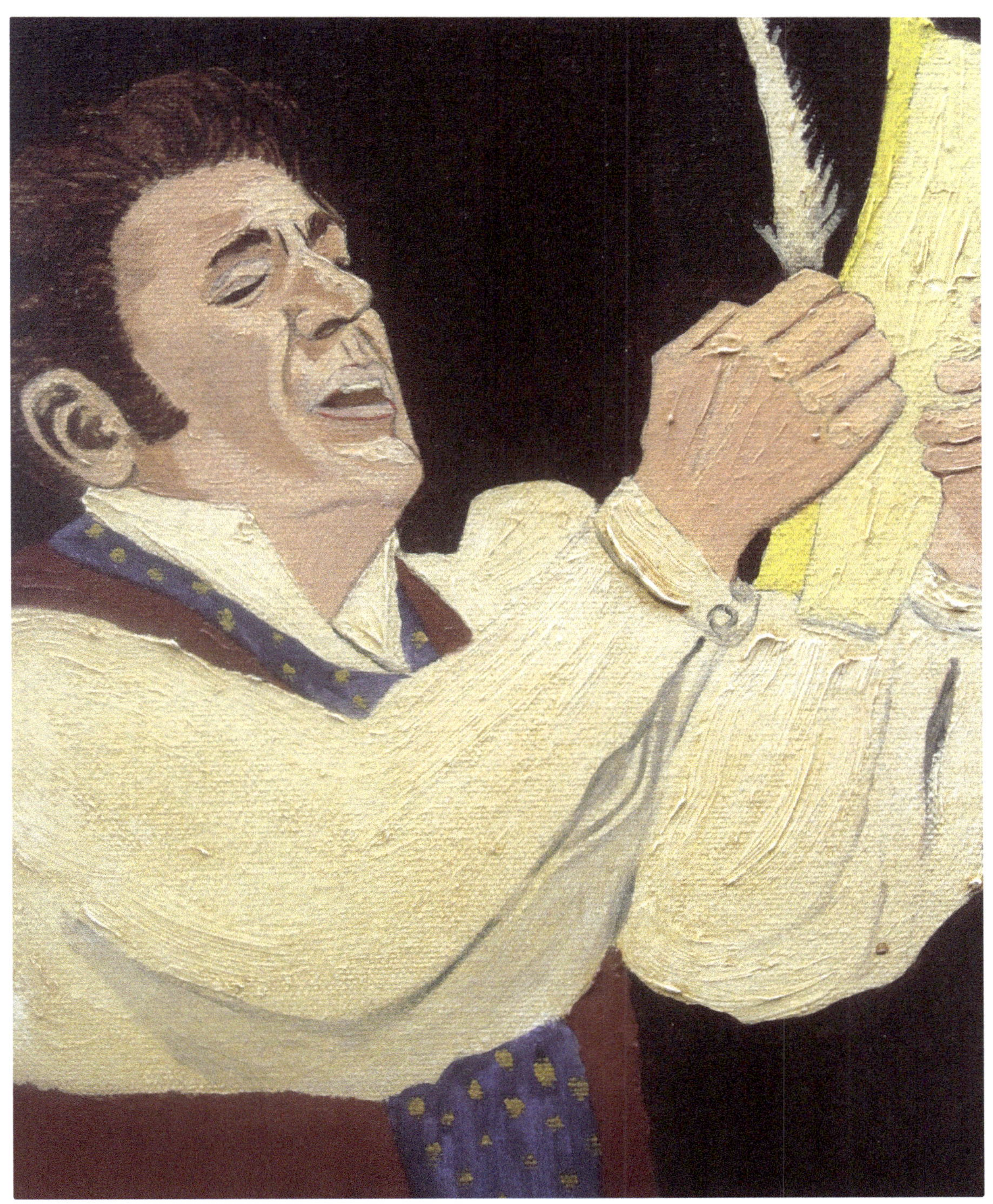

SIR GERAINT EVANS
Baritone

Born in Pontypridd, South Wales, 1922; died in Aberystwyth, South Wales, 1992. Debut as Night Watchman (*Meistersinger*), 1948, Covent Garden, where he sang Figaro in 1949. From 1950 to 1961 he sang regularly at Glyndbourne. Other debuts: San Francisco (Beckmesser) 1959, La Scala (Figaro) 1960, Salzburg (Figaro) 1962, The Met (Falstaff) 1964, Paris (Leporello) 1975. He created many parts in British operas, particularly the works of Britten, but was best known for the roles that he made his debuts in and for Papageno.

Geraint Evans as Papageno
(*Die Zauberfloete*)

Die Zauberfloete, opera in 2 acts by **Wolfgang Amadeus Mozart**, first performed in Vienna, 1791.

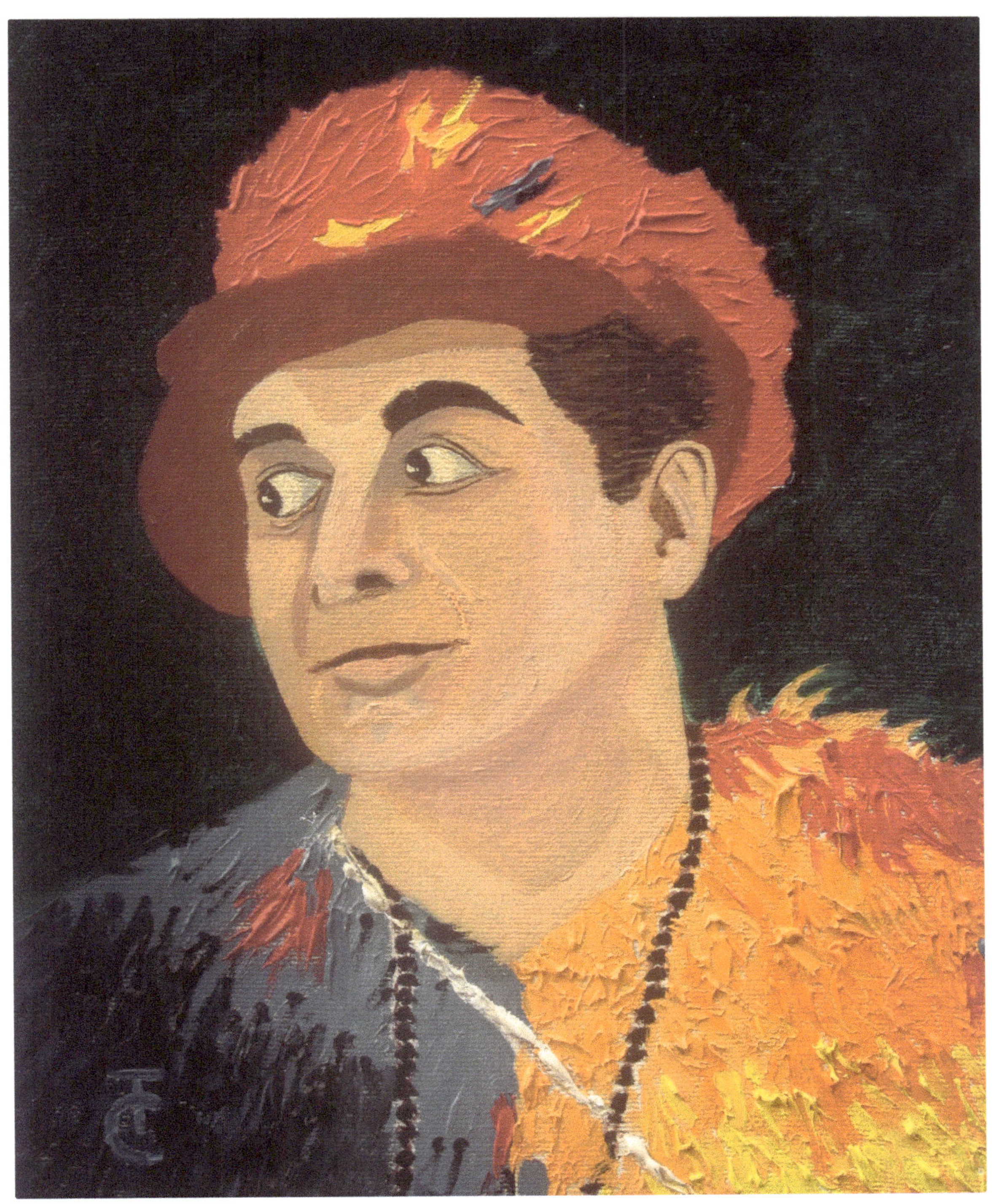

KIRSTEN FLAGSTAD
Dramatic Soprano

Born in Hamar, Norway, 1895; died in Oslo, Norway, 1962.
Debut: Oslo (National Theatre), 1913, as Nuri (*Tiefland*).
From 1913 to 1933 she appeared only in Scandinavia. Other
debuts: *Bayreuth* (1933-34) as Gutrune (*Goetterdaemmerung*)
and Sieglinde (*Die Walkuere*); the Met (1935) as Sieglinde;
San Francisco (1935) as Bruennhilde in the company's first
complete production of *Der Ring des Nibelungen*; and Covent
Garden (1936) as Isolde (*Tristan und Isolde*). She did not
resume her career in America after the war until 1949,
when she returned to San Francisco. She was the
pre-eminent Wagnerian soprano of her generation.

Kirsten Flagstad as Isolde
(*Tristan und Isolde*)

Tristan und Isolde, opera in 3 acts by **Richard Wagner**,
first performed in Munich, Hoftheater, 1865.

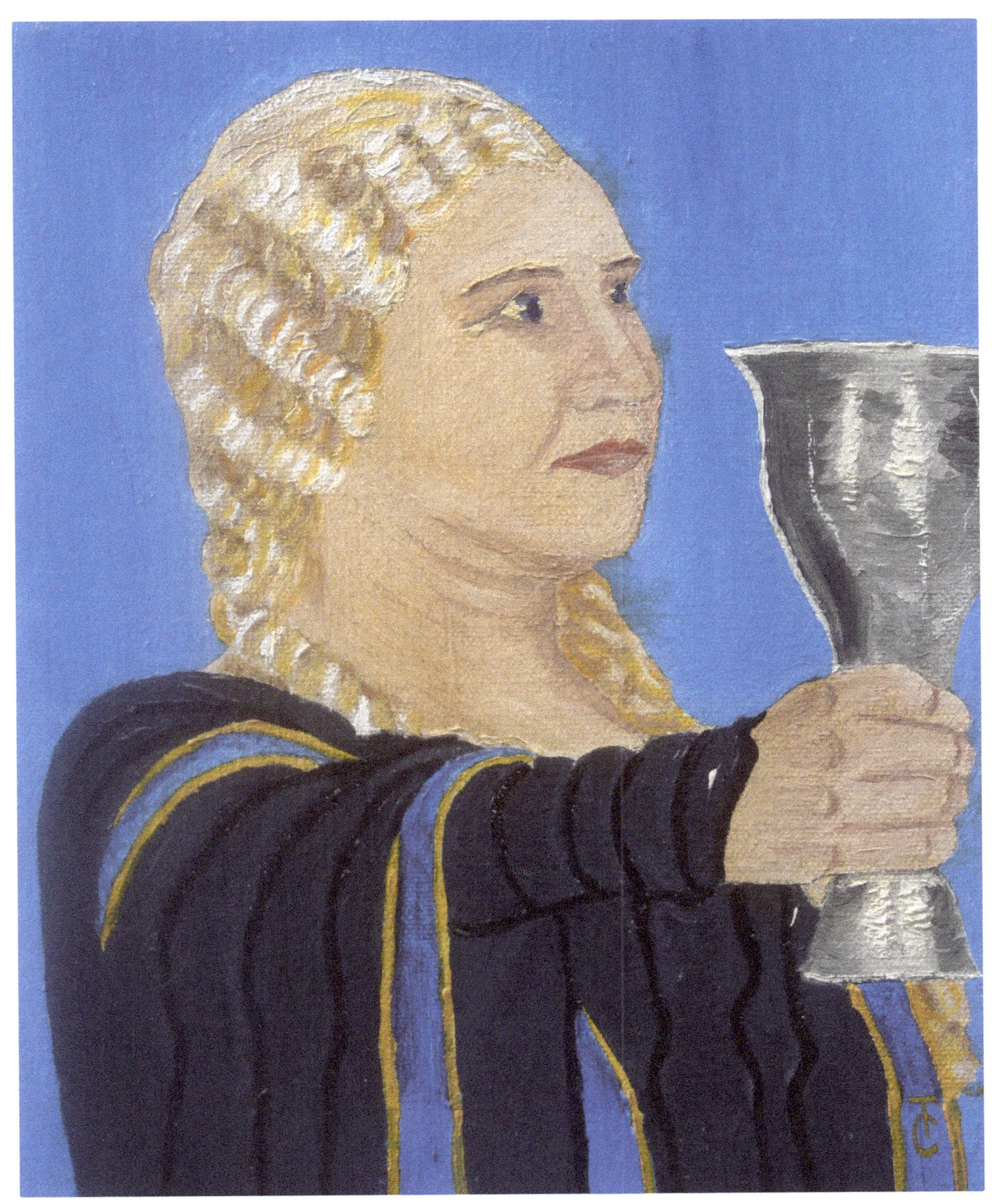

DIETRICH FISCHER-DIESKAU
Baritone

Born in Zehlendorf, Germany, 1925; died in Bavaria, Germany, 2012.
Debut: Berlin (Stadtische Oper) 1948, as Posa (*Don Carlos*). He
developed a wide repertoire of roles in the operas of
Mozart, Gluck, Verdi, Wagner, Strauss, Busoni, Berg
and Hindemith while maintaining a career as the
pre-eminent concert singer of his generation. He
created roles in several new operas including
Henze's *Elegy for Young Lovers*.

Dietrich Fischer-Dieskau as Rodrigo
(*Don Carlos*)

Don Carlos, opera in 4 acts by **Giuseppe Verdi**,
first performed in Paris, 1867.

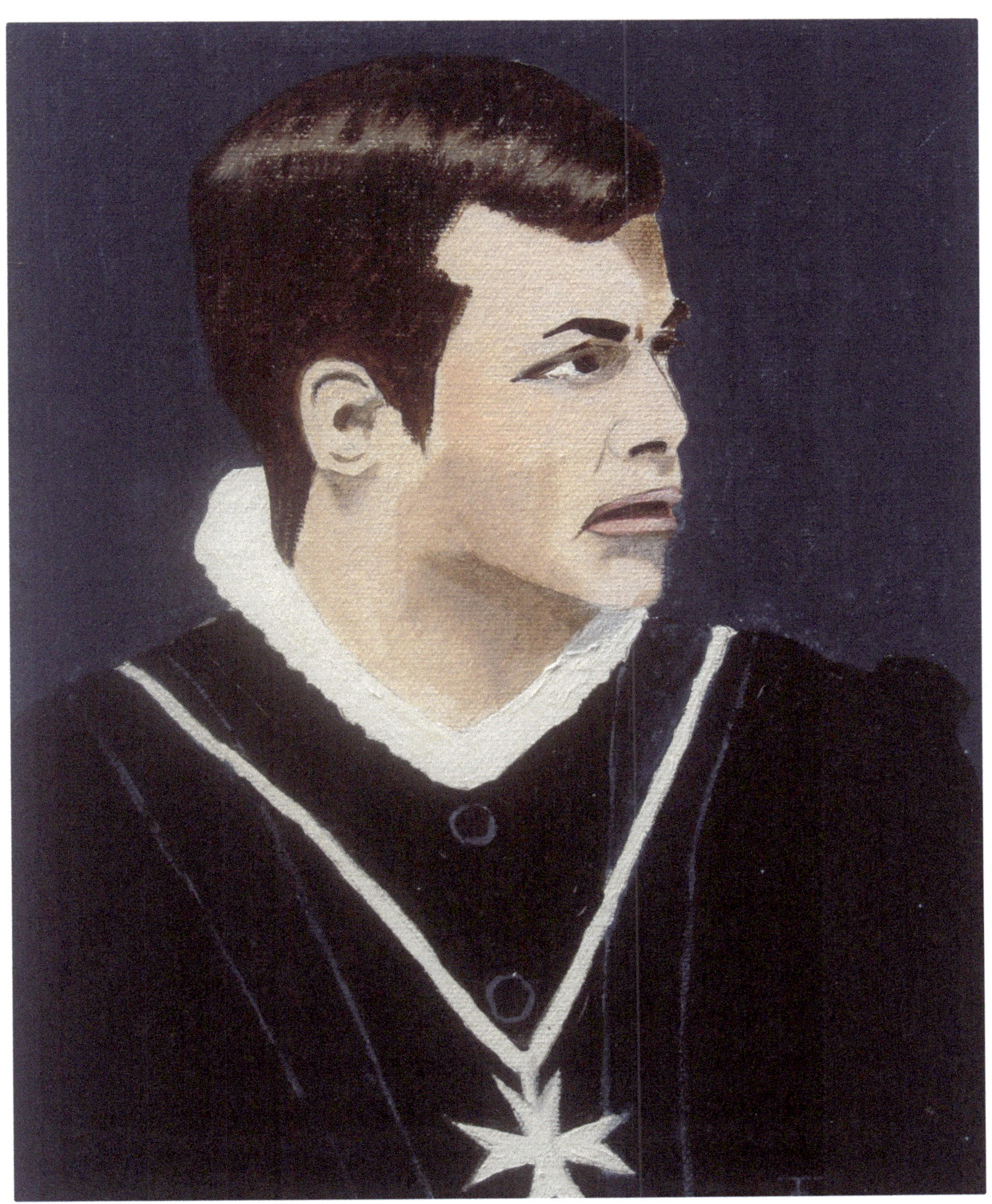

AMELITA GALLI-CURCI
Soprano

Born in Milan, Italy, 1882; died in La Jolla, California,
1963. Debuts: Trani (1906), Rome (1910), and Chicago (1916),
in each performance as Gilda (*Rigoletto*). She had successes in Spain,
Russia and South America and was a star in Chicago from 1916 until
1924. She had her debut at the Met in 1921 as Violetta (*La Traviata*)
and performed there until 1930. She is considered to be one of the
finest recording artists of the early 20th century.

Amelita Galli-Curci as Rosina
(*Il Barbieri di Siviglia*)

Il Barbieri di Siviglia, opera buffo in 2 acts by **Gioacchino Rossini**,
first performed in Rome, Teatro Argentina, 1816.

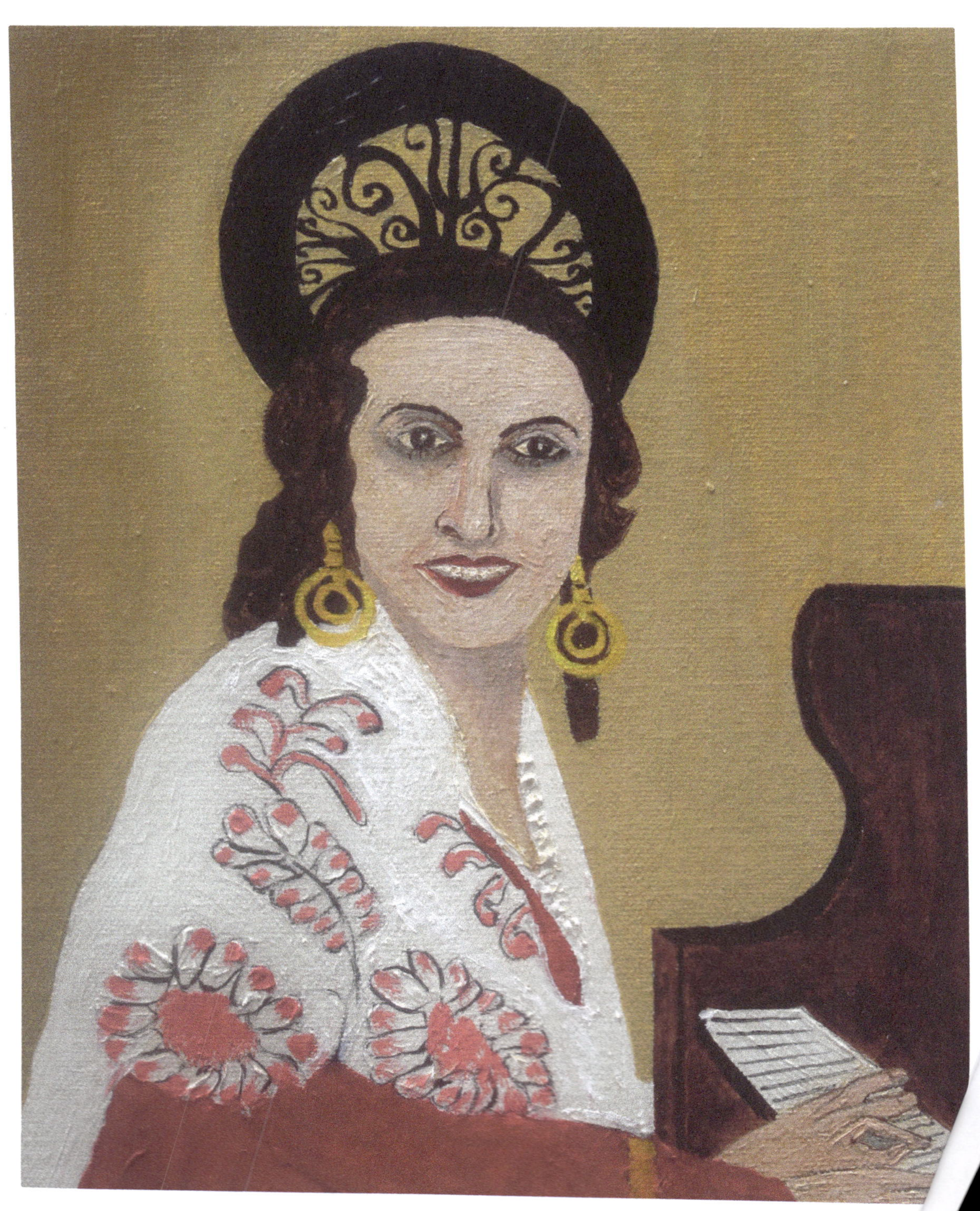

MARY GARDEN
Soprano

Born in Aberdeen, Scotland, 1874; died in Inverurie, Scotland, 1967. Her unscheduled debut occurred in 1900 when she replaced an indisposed colleague at Paris's Opera-Comique in Charpentier's *Louise*, to instant acclaim. She created the role of Mélisande (*Pelléas et Mélisande* by Debussy) at Opéra-Comique in 1902. She made her debut in London and Monte Carlo in 1904 and in New York in 1907 with Hammerstein's Manhatten Opera, in the first U.S. production of *Thais*. In 1910 she began a 20-year association with Chicago Opera, which included a season (1920-21) as the company's artistic director. A versatile lyric soprano, Garden was also reputedly a superlative actress.

Mary Garden as Thais
(*Thais*)

Thais, opera in 3 acts by **Jules Massenet**, first performed by **Paris** Opera in 1894.

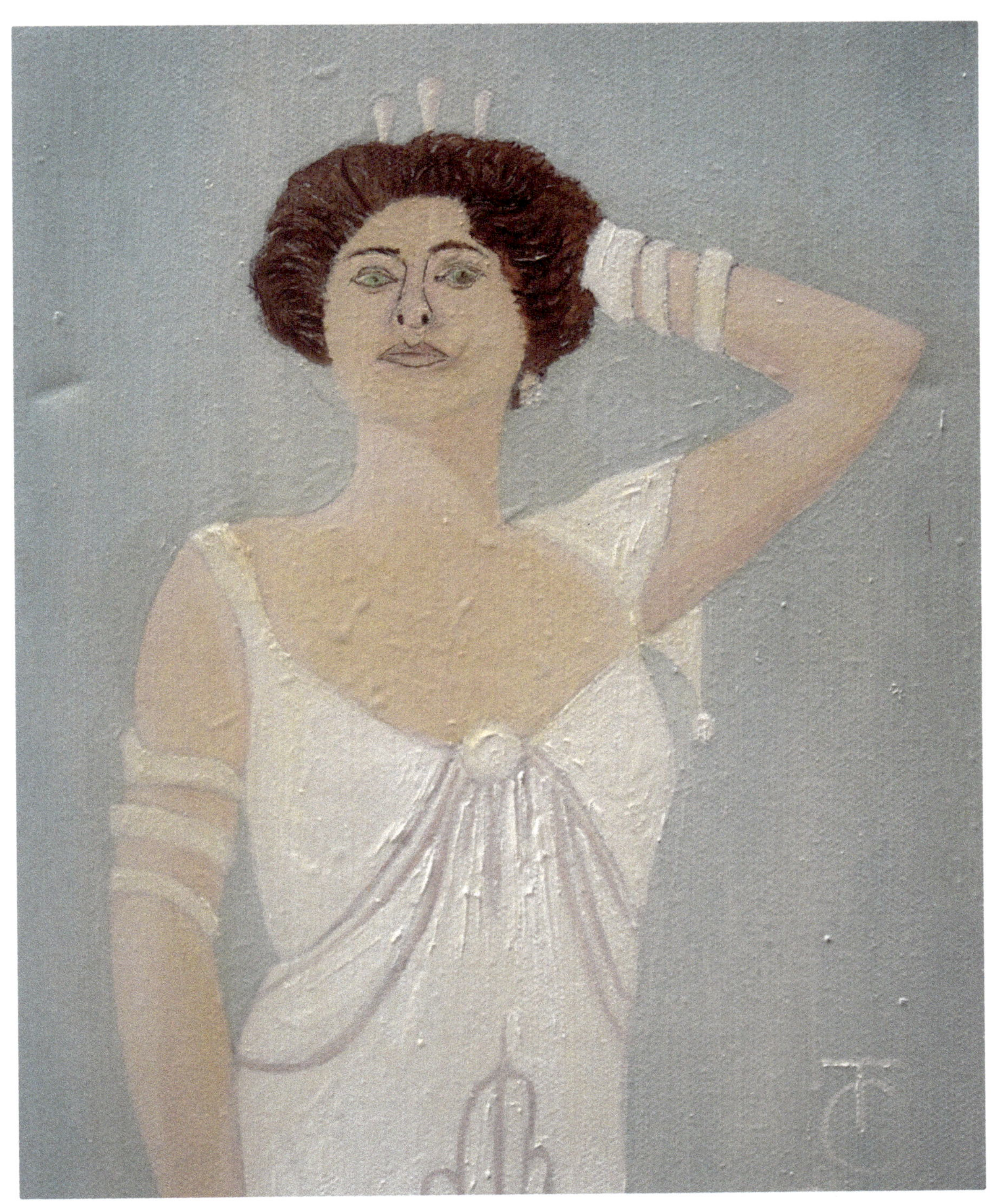

NICOLAI GHIAUROV
Bass

Born in Velingrad, Bulgaria, 1929; died in Modena, Italy, 2004. Debut as Basilio (*Il Barbiere di Siviglia*) 1955 in Sofia, then with the Bolshoi in Moscow as Pimen (*Boris Godunov*) 1958. Other debuts: La Scala, 1960 as Varlaam (*Boris*); Covent Garden, 1962, as Padre Guardiano (*La Forza del Destino*); Chicago, 1963, as Mephistopheles (*Faust*); and in 1965 the Met as Mephistopheles and in Salzburg as Boris. A master of the great Russian roles, he is also acclaimed as the pre-eminent Don Giovanni and Philippe II of his generation.

Nicolai Ghiaurov as Philippe II
(*Don Carlos*)

Don Carlos, opera in 4 acts by **Giuseppi Verdi**,
first performed in Paris, 1867.

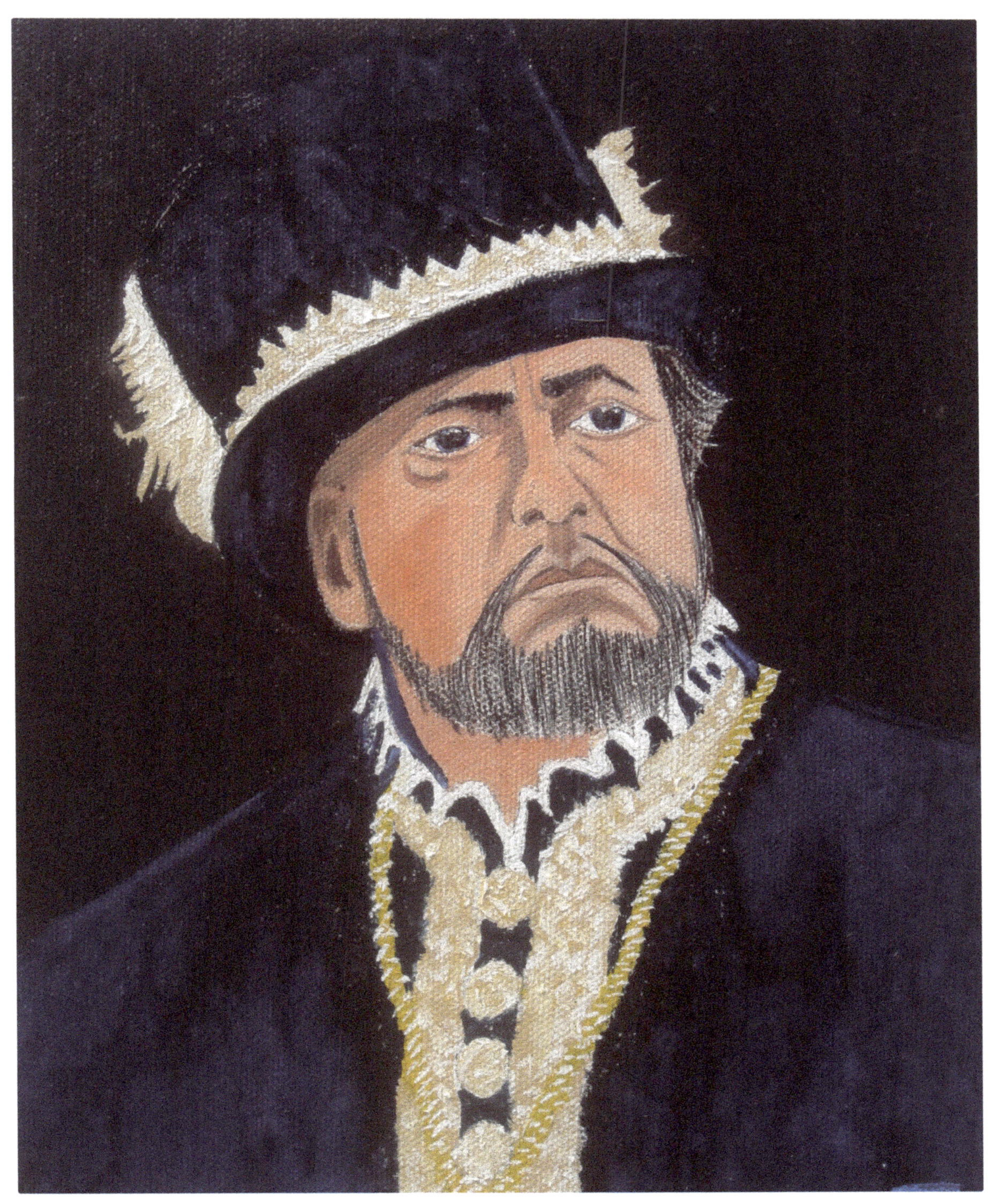

BENIAMINO GIGLI
Lyric Tenor

Born in Recanati, Italy, 1890; died in Rome, Italy, 1957.
Debut: Rovigo, 1914, as Enzo (*La Gioconda*). He had notable
successes as Boito's Faust (*Mefistofele*) at Bologna under Serafin,
Naples under Mascagni and at La Scala under Toscanini, each
performance in 1918, before his Met debut in the same role in 1920.
He sang every season at the Met until 1932. He had a particularly
mellifluous voice, which has been preserved in many recordings.

Beniamino Gigli as Vasco da Gama
(*L'Africaine*)

L'Africaine, opera in 5 acts by **Giacomo Meyerbeer**,
first performed in Paris in 1865.

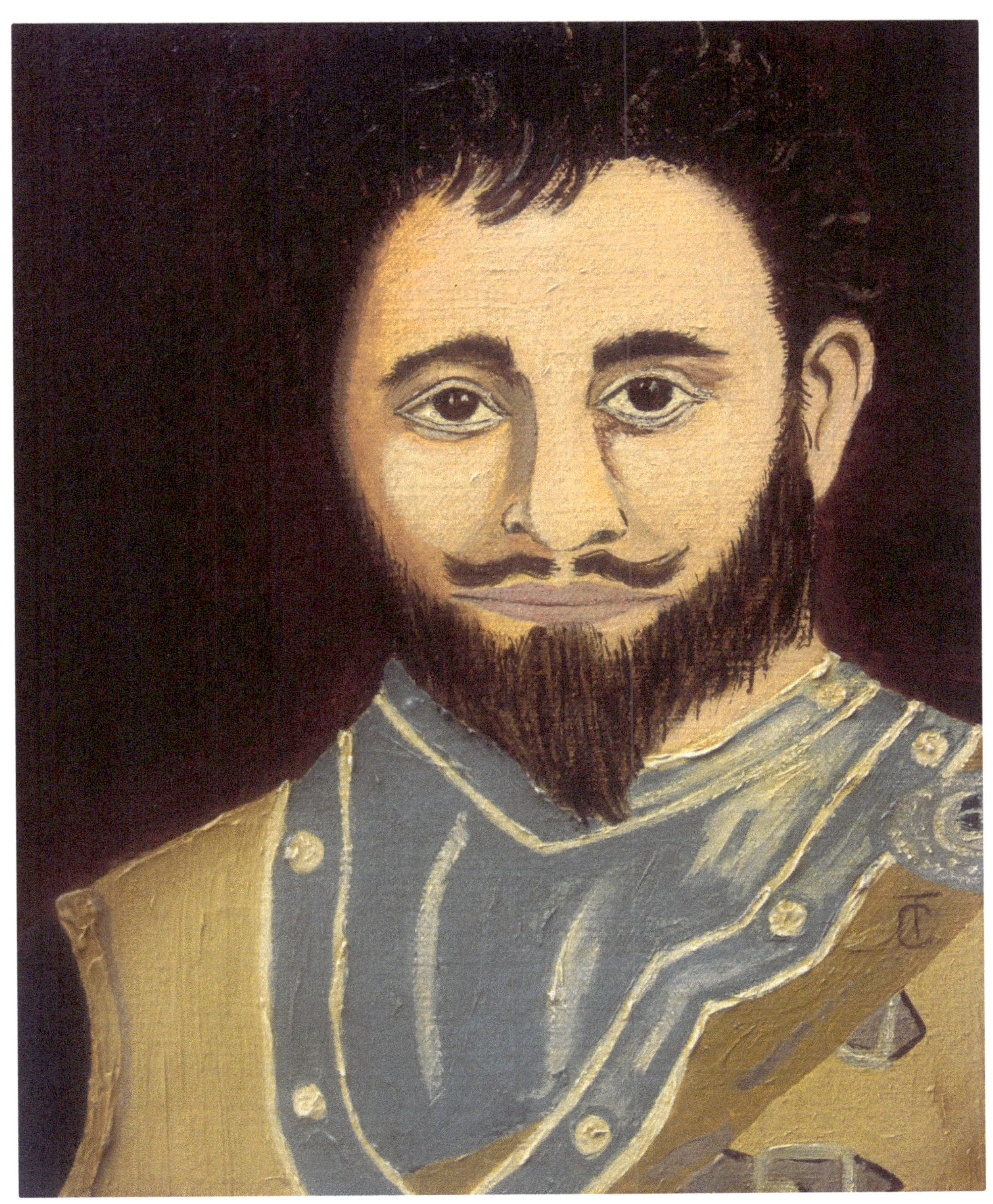

TITO GOBBI
Baritone

Born in Bassano del Grappa, Italy, 1913; died in
Rome, Italy, 1984. Debut as Rodolfo (*La Sonnambula*)
in Gubbio, 1935. He made his debut at La Scala in 1942
as Belcore (*L'Elisir d'Amore*). His U.S. debut was with San
Francisco Opera in 1948 as Rossini's Figaro. In 1954, he
appeared with Chicago Lyric Opera, where he continued to
perform through 1973. His Met debut as Scarpia was in 1956.
Like his great predecessor, Giuseppe de Luca, he dominated
the Italian repertoire of his own generation by bolstering his
fine baritone voice with a combination of intelligence,
personality and acting ability.

Tito Gobbi as Scarpia
(*Tosca*)

Tosca, opera in 3 acts by **Giacomo Puccini**,
first performed in Rome, Teatro Costanza, 1900.

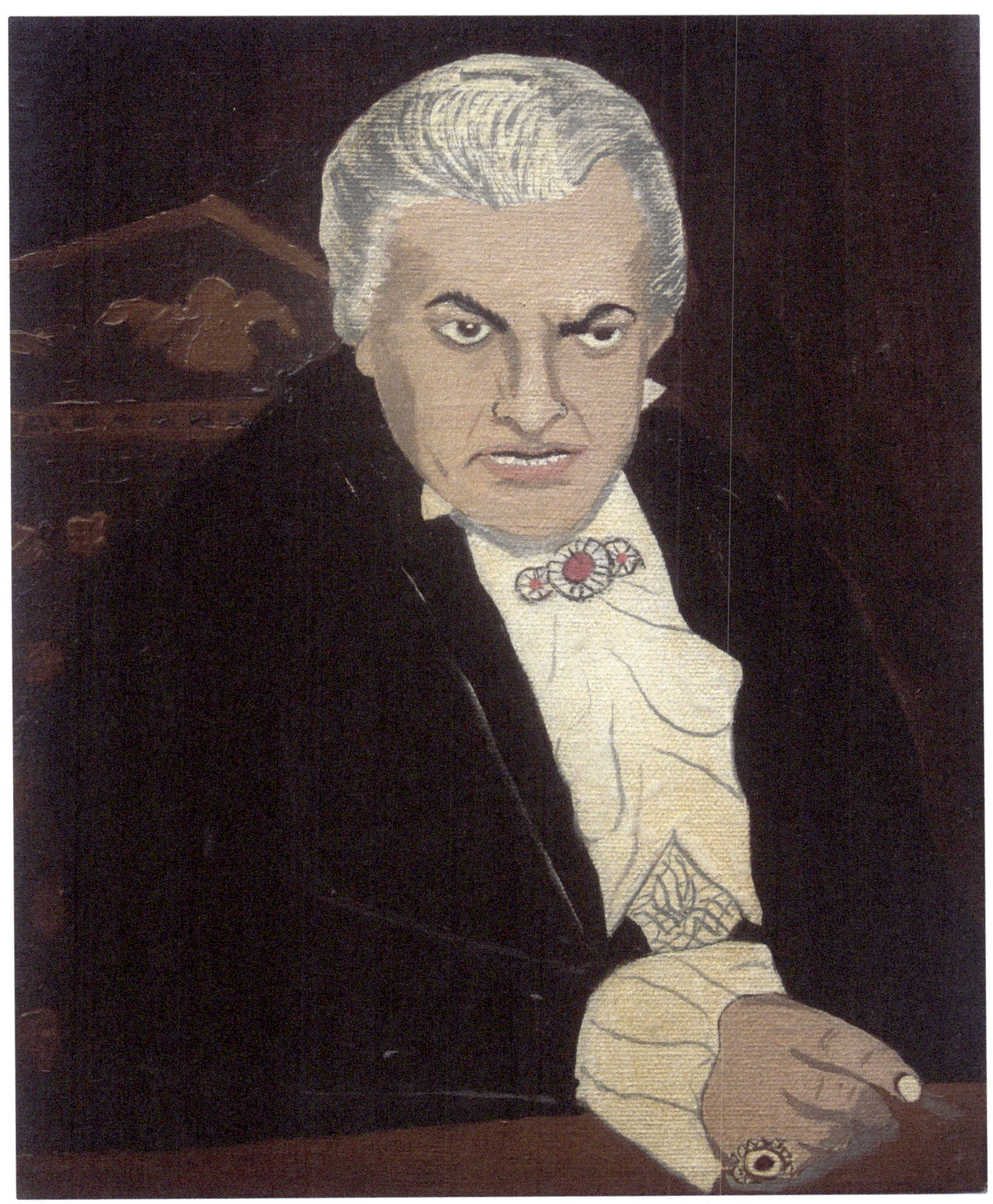

MARILYN HORNE
Mezzo

Born in Bradford, Pennsylvania, 1934. Debut as Hata (*The Bartered Bride*) Los Angeles Guild Opera, 1954, the same year she dubbed Dorothy Dandridge's voice for the movie *Carmen Jones*. Debuts in major houses: San Francisco, 1960, as Marie (*Wozzeck*); Chicago, 1961, as Lora in Giannini's *The Harvest*; Covent Garden, 1964, *Wozzeck*; La Scala, 1969 Jocasta in *Oedipus Rex*; the Met, 1970, as Adalgisa in *Norma* opposite Joan Sutherland. While commanding a wide repertoire, she distinguished herself by mastering infrequently performed operas of Rossini and the Baroque period.

Marilyn Horne as Isabella
(*L'Italiana in Algeri*)

L' Italiana in Algeri, opera in 2 acts by **Gioacchino Rossini**, first performed in Venice, 1813.

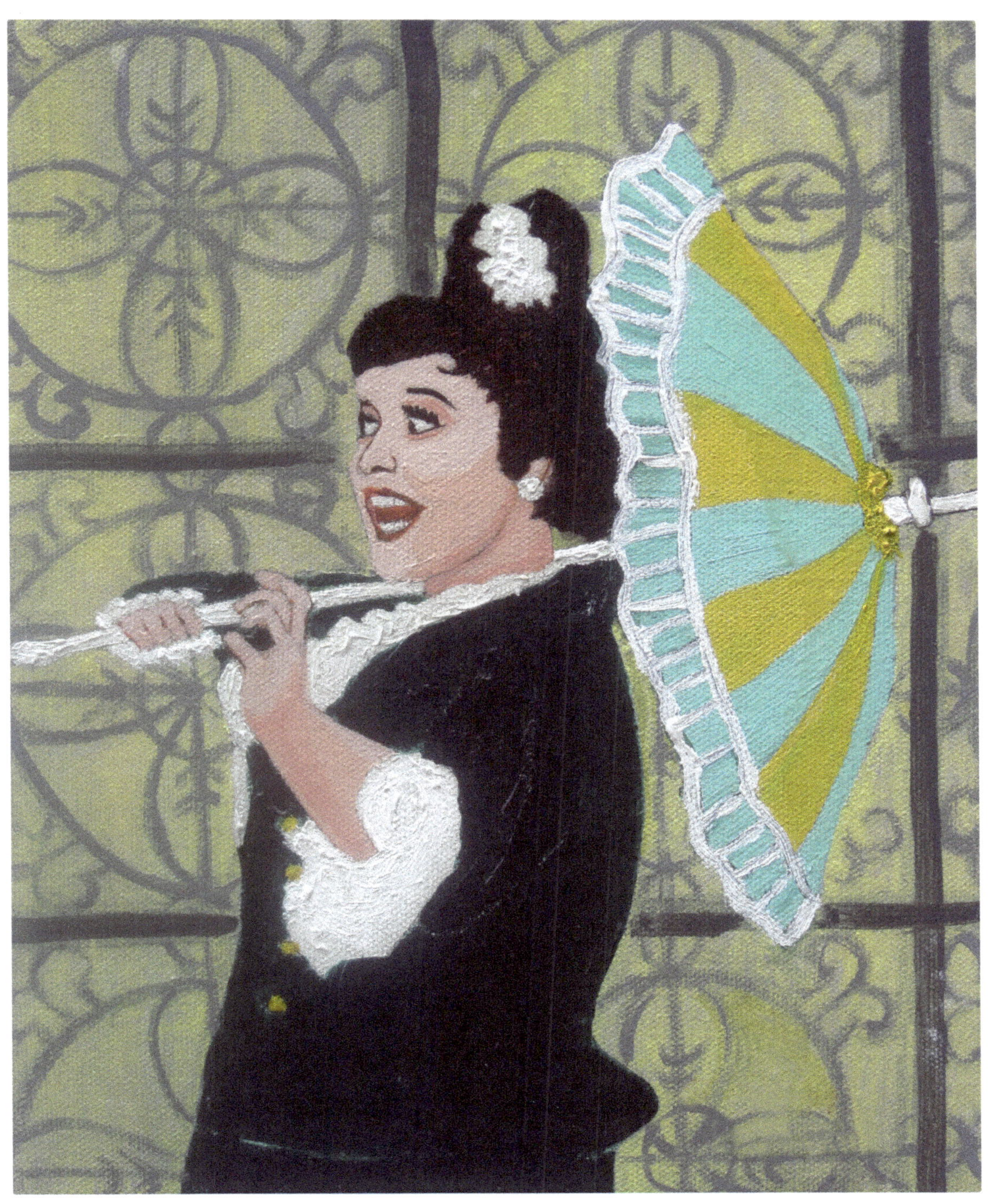

HANS HOTTER
Bass-Baritone

Born in Offenbach am Main, Germany, 1909, died in Gruenwald, Germany, 2003. Debut in Troppau, 1930, then engagements in Prague (1932-34), Hamburg (1934-45), Munich from 1934, Berlin and Vienna, from 1939, until his retirement. Closely associated with Richard Strauss, he created Olivier (*Capriccio*) in 1942. He made his Met debut in 1950 as the Dutchman and was the outstanding Wotan of post-war Bayreuth productions. His repertoire of 110 roles included many in 20th century German operas as well as standard works by Verdi, Mozart and Puccini.

Hans Hotter as Amfortas
(*Parsifal*)

Parsifal, opera in 3 acts by **Richard Wagner**,
first performed at Bayreuth in 1882.

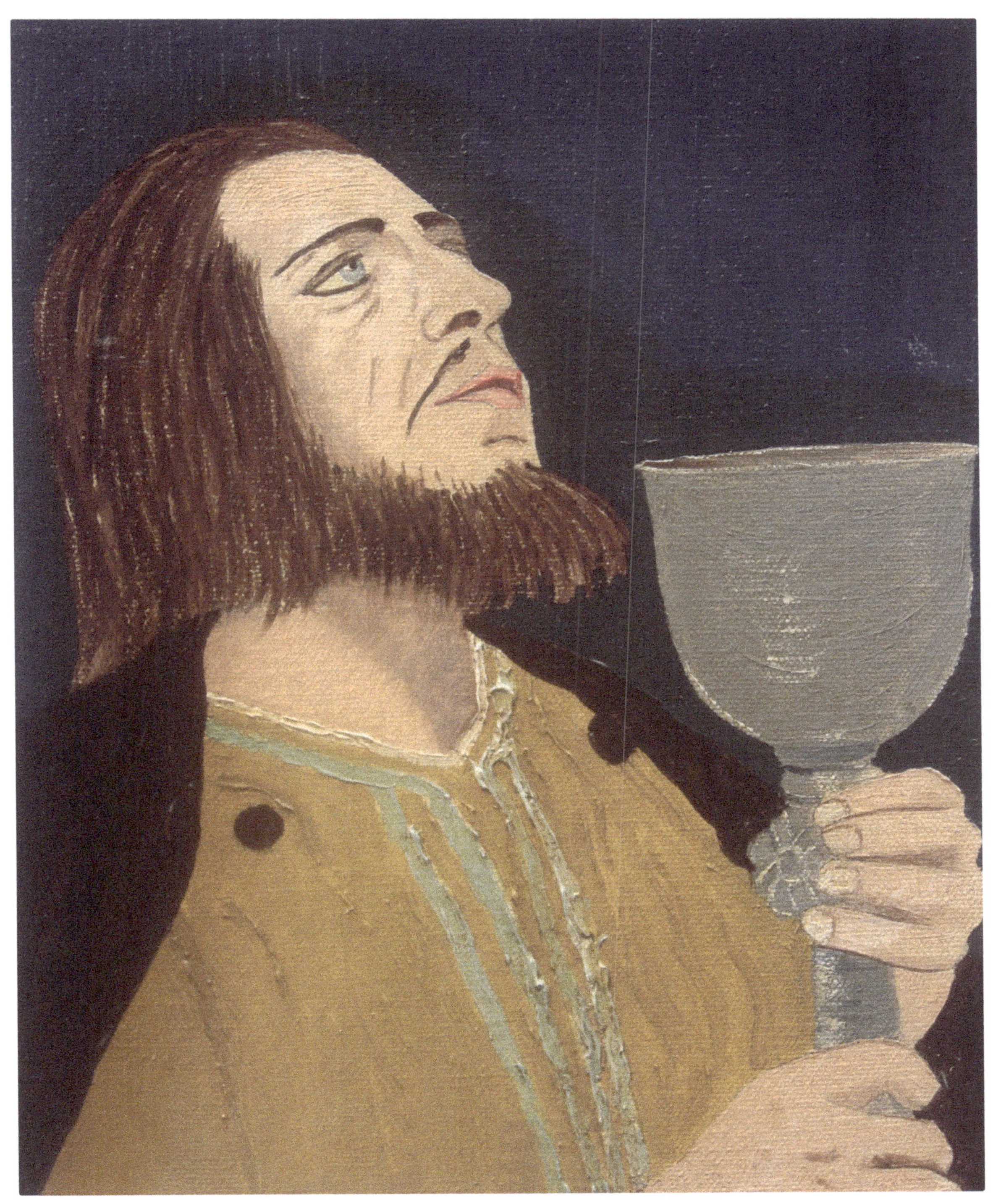

M A R I A   J E R I T Z A
Soprano

Born in Brno, Moravia, in 1887; died in Orange, New Jersey, 1982.
Debuts: Olomouc, 1910, as Elsa (*Lohengrin*); Vienna, 1911,
as Elizabeth (*Tannhaeuser*). She created Strauss's Ariadne
(*Ariadne auf Naxos*) in Stuttgart, 1912, and the Empress
(*Die Frau ohne Schatten*) in Vienna, 1919. She had her
debut at the Met in 1921 and for a dozen years
thereafter was unrivalled in German roles
and as Tosca and Turandot.

Maria Jeritza as Jenufa
(*Jenufa*)

Jenufa, opera in 3 acts by **Leos Janacek**,
first performed in Brno, 1904.

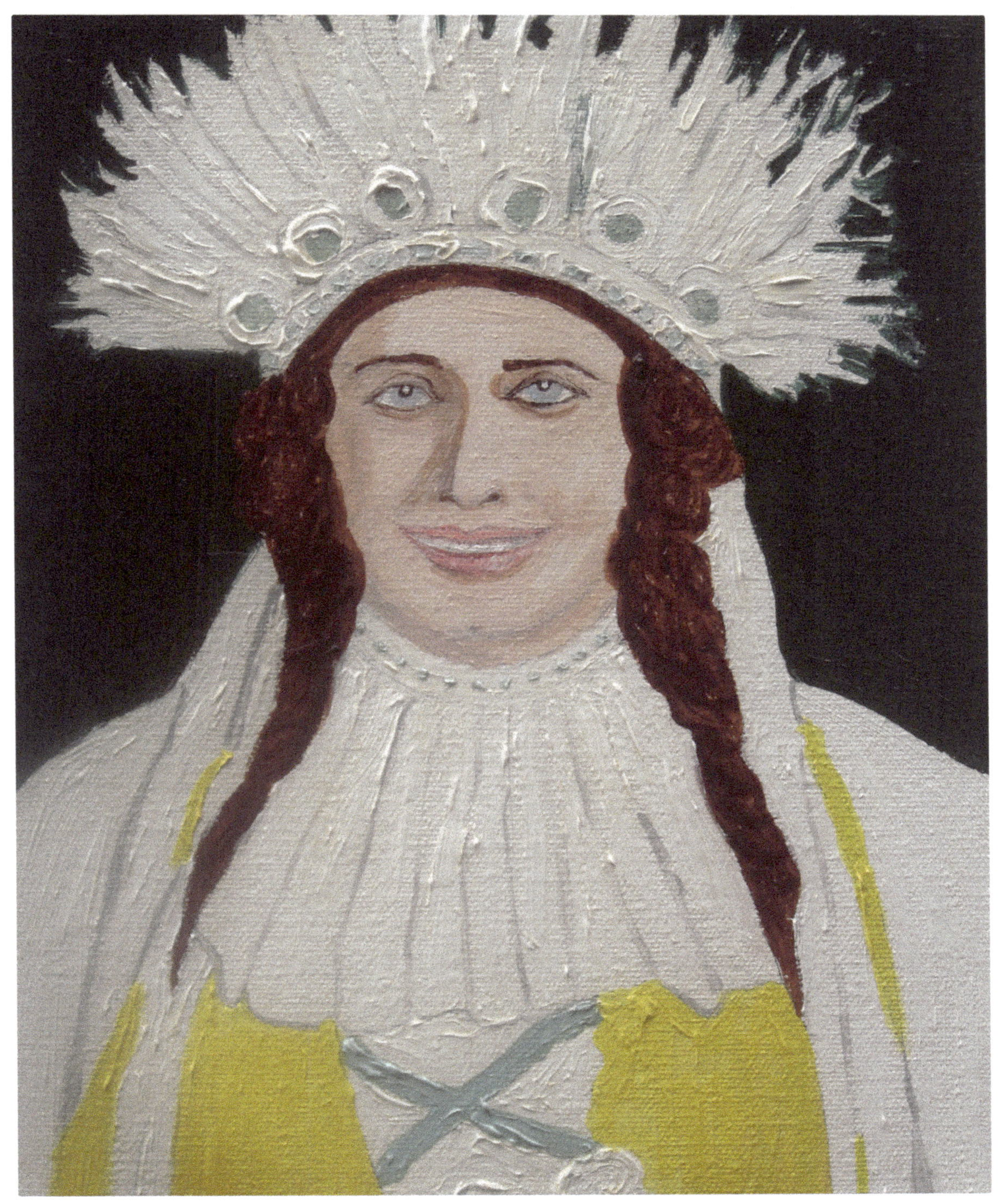

49

ALEXANDER KIPNIS
Bass

Born in Zhitomir, Ukraine, 1891; died in Westport, Connecticut, 1978.
Debut in Hamburg, Germany, 1915. He was the leading bass at Berlin
Charlottenburg Oper (1919-1929) and at State Opera (1930-35). U.S.
debut as Pogner (*Die Meistersinger*) in Baltimore (1923). He sang in
Chicago (1923-32) and had his Met debut as Gurnemanz (*Parsifal*)
in 1940. He sang 13 roles in 7 seasons at the Met, including his
celebrated Boris in Russian, which he sang only twice, in 1943.

Alexander Kipnis as Gurnemanz
(*Parsifal*)

Parsifal, opera in 3 acts by **Richard Wagner**,
first performed at Bayreuth in 1882.

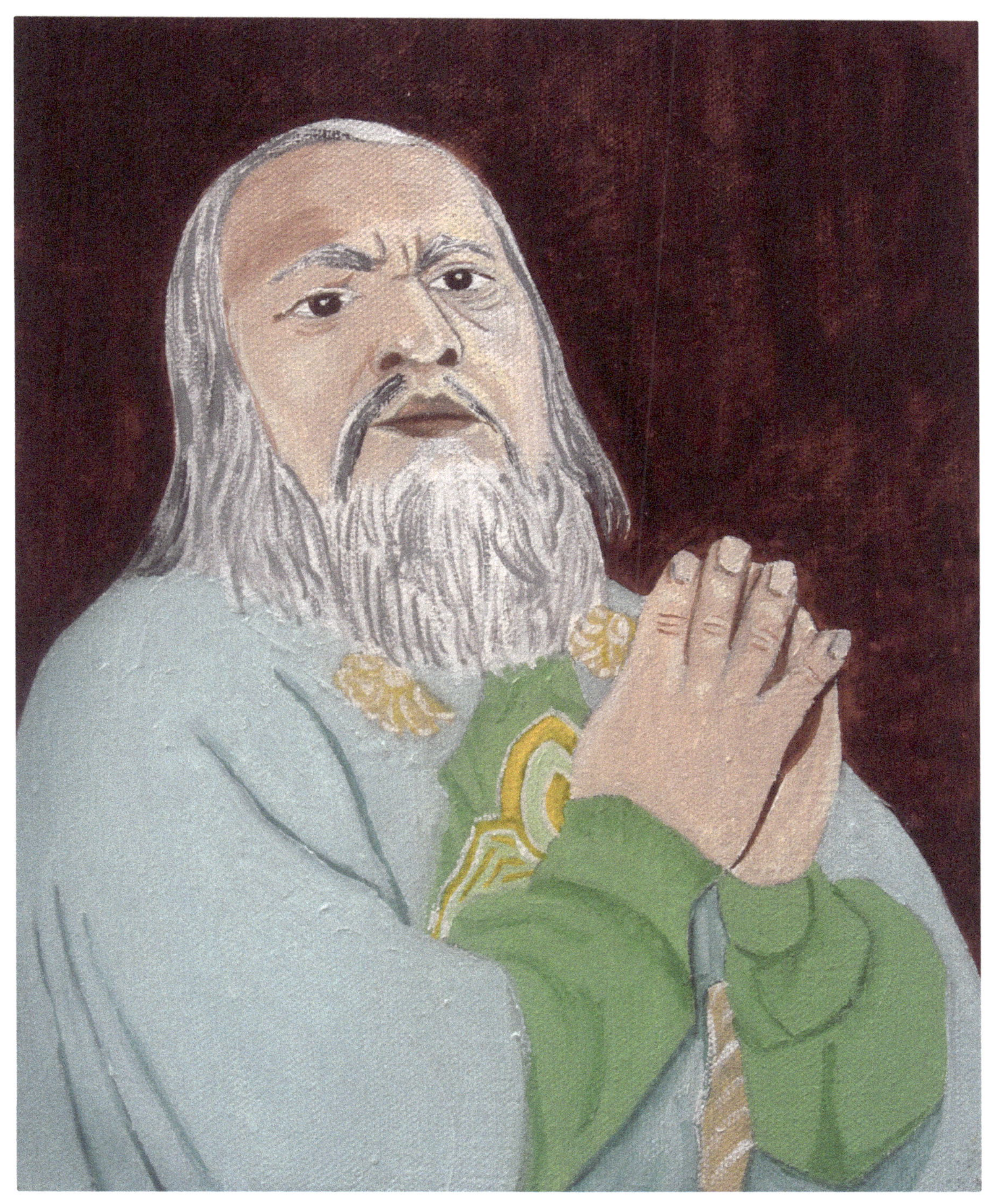

LILLI LEHMANN
Soprano

Born in Wurzburg, Germany, 1848; died in Berlin, Germany, 1929. She made her debut in Prague as First Boy (*The Magic Flute*) in 1865. She first sang in Berlin in *Les Huguenots* in 1869 and in Bayreuth in 1876. The extraordinarily versatile soprano made her debut in London as Violetta (*La Traviata*) in 1880 and at the Met as Carmen in 1885. She sang 25 different roles at the Met in 7 seasons. Though she began as a coloratura she became the pre-eminent Wagnerian heroic soprano of her day. Lehmann performed for 45 years, reputedly singing 170 roles.

Lilli Lehmann as Bruennhilde
(*Die Walkuere*)

Die Walkuere, opera in 3 acts (the second of four operas in Ring cycle), by **Richard Wagner**, first performed in Munich in 1870.

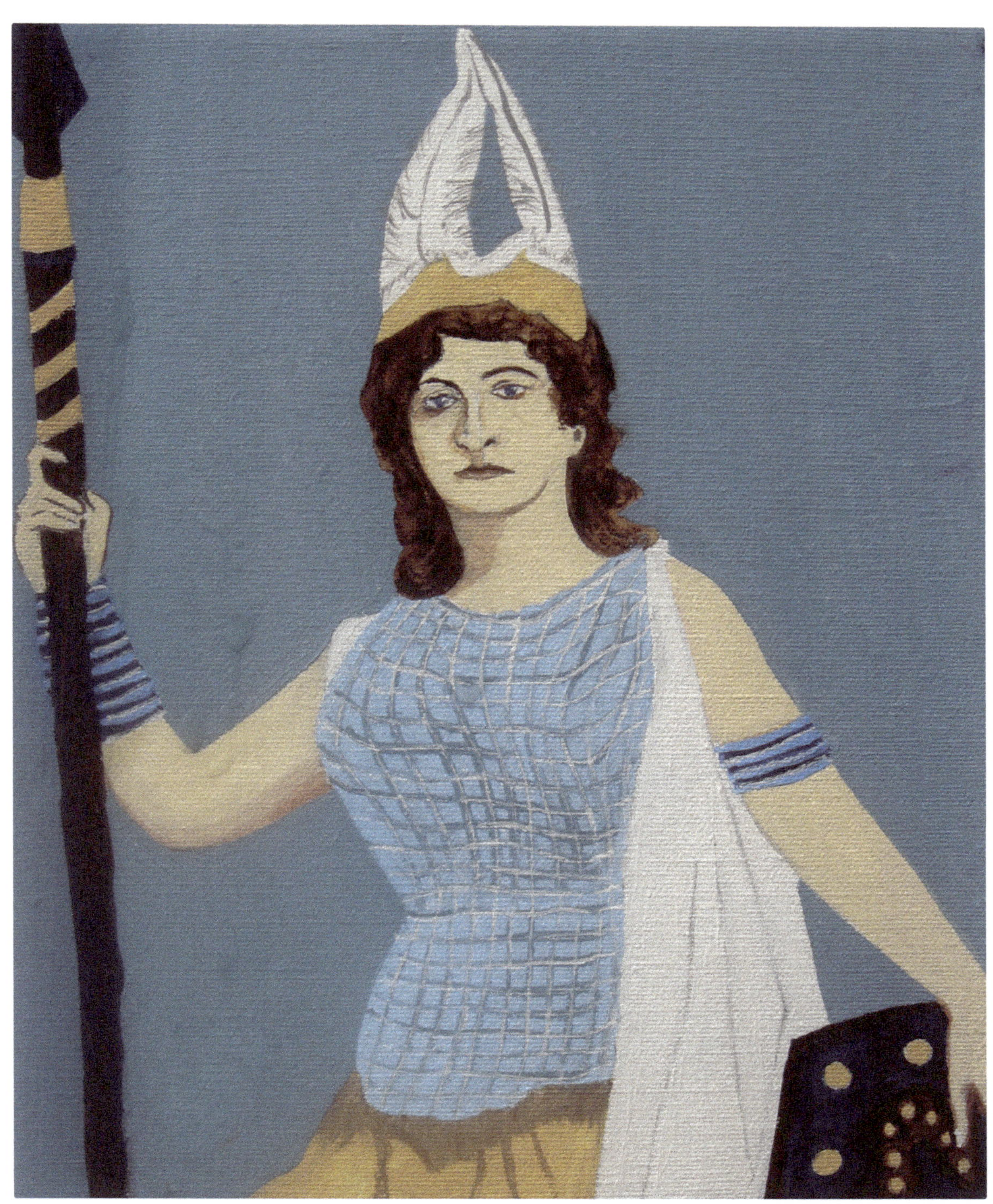

LOTTE LEHMANN
Soprano

Born in Perleberg, Germany, 1888; died in Santa Barbara, California, 1976. Debuts: Hamburg, 1910, in *Die Zauberfloete*; Vienna, 1916; Covent Garden, 1924; Salzberg 1927; Chicago, 1930; the Met as Sieglinde (*Die Walkuere*), 1934; and San Francisco, 1946. She was engaged for twenty years at the Vienna Hofoper, where she was known especially for her interpretations of Richard Strauss roles, several of which she created. She became a U.S. citizen in 1945 and was a highly influential singing teacher in her adopted country.

Lotte Lehmann as Sieglinde
(*Die Walkuere*)

Die Walkuere, opera in 3 acts by **Richard Wagner**, first performed in Munich, 1870.

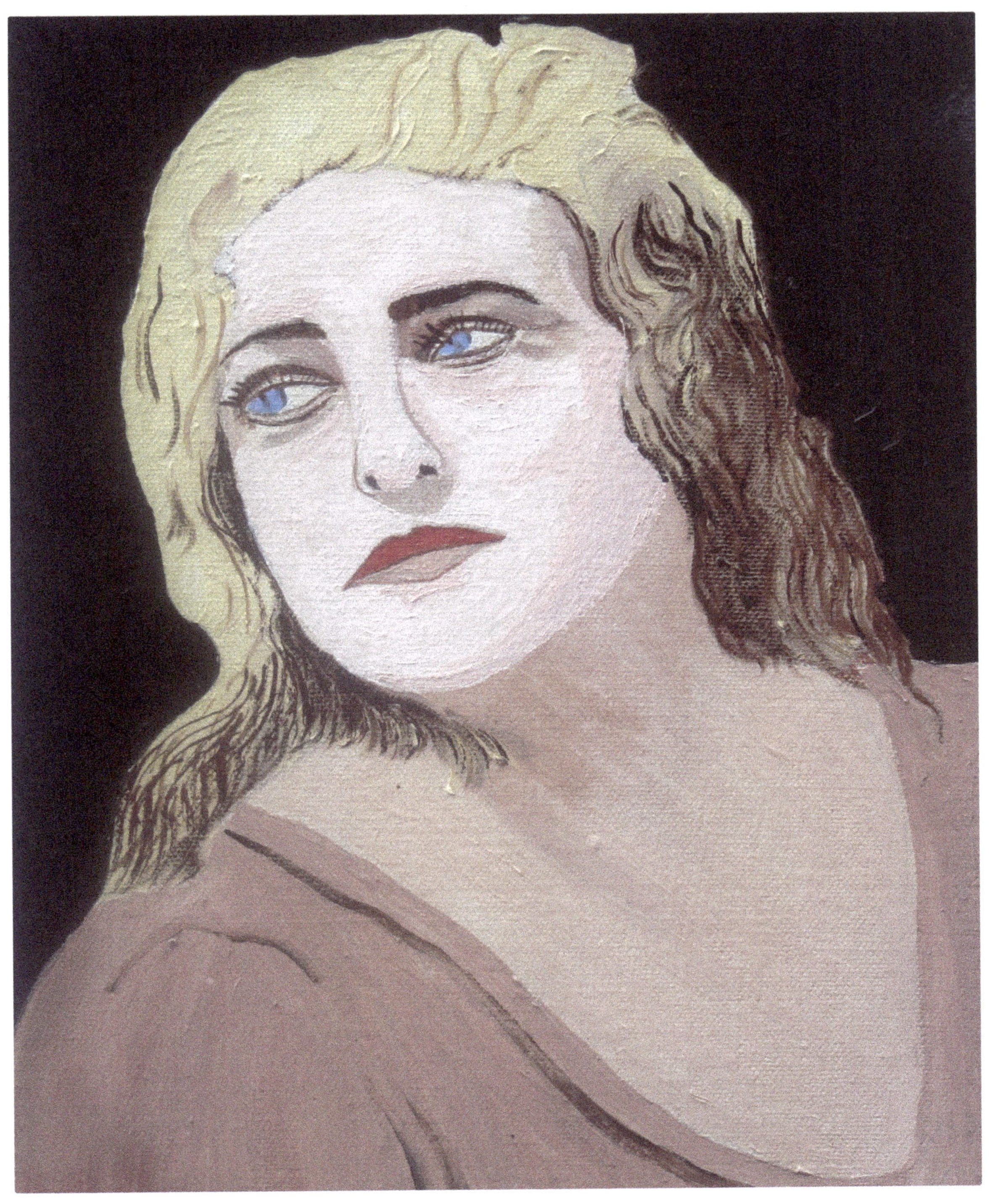

JOHN McCORMACK
Tenor

Born in Athlone, Ireland, 1884; died in Dublin, Ireland, 1945. Debuts: Savona, Italy as Fritz (*L'amico Fritz*), 1906; Covent Garden, as Turiddu (*Cavalleria rusticana*), 1907; Chicago as Turiddu and the Met as Alfredo (*La Traviata*) both in 1910. His last operatic appearances were in 1923 but he continued to sing recitals until 1938. His widely criticized undramatic stage presence could not diminish the glory of his sweet voice, elegant phrasing and impeccable Italianate sound.

John McCormack as Rodolfo
(*La Bohème*)

La Bohème, opera in 4 acts by **Giacomo Puccini**, first performed in Turin, Teatro Regio, 1896.

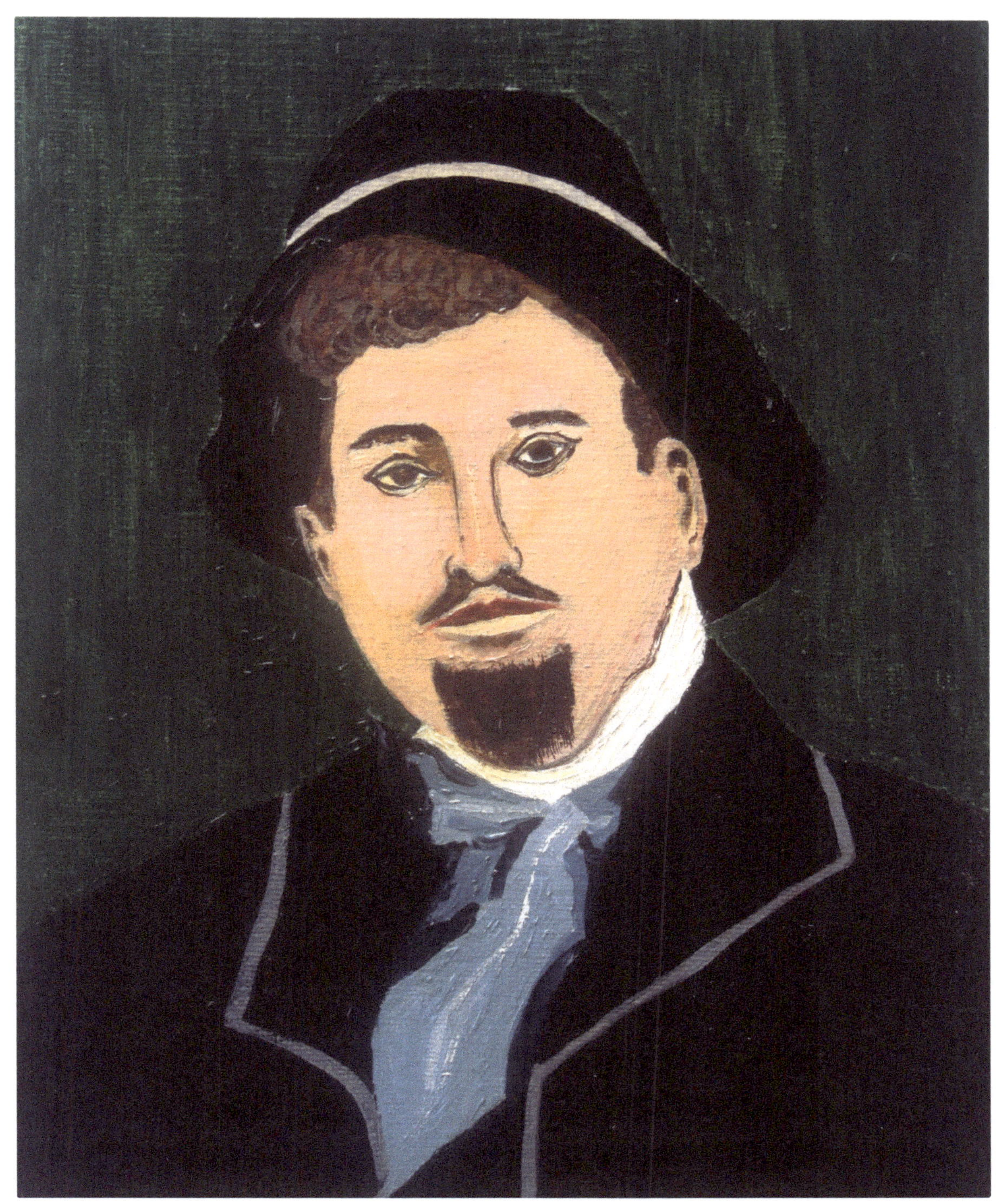

DAME NELLIE MELBA
Coloratura Soprano

Born in Richmond, Australia, 1861; died in Sydney, Australia, 1931.
Debuts: Brussels, 1887, as Gilda (*Rigoletto*); 1888, Covent Garden, as
Lucia (*Lucia di Lammermoor*); La Scala and the Met, both in 1893.
Her repertoire was limited but she was reknowned as an unparalleled
vocal technician. In 1922 she founded the British National Opera
Company and then organized a company to tour Australia. Her
popularity throughout the British Commonwealth was enormous.

Nellie Melba as Marguerite
(*Faust*)

Faust, opera in 5 acts by **Charles Gounod**,
first performed at Paris, Théâtre-Lyrique, 1859.

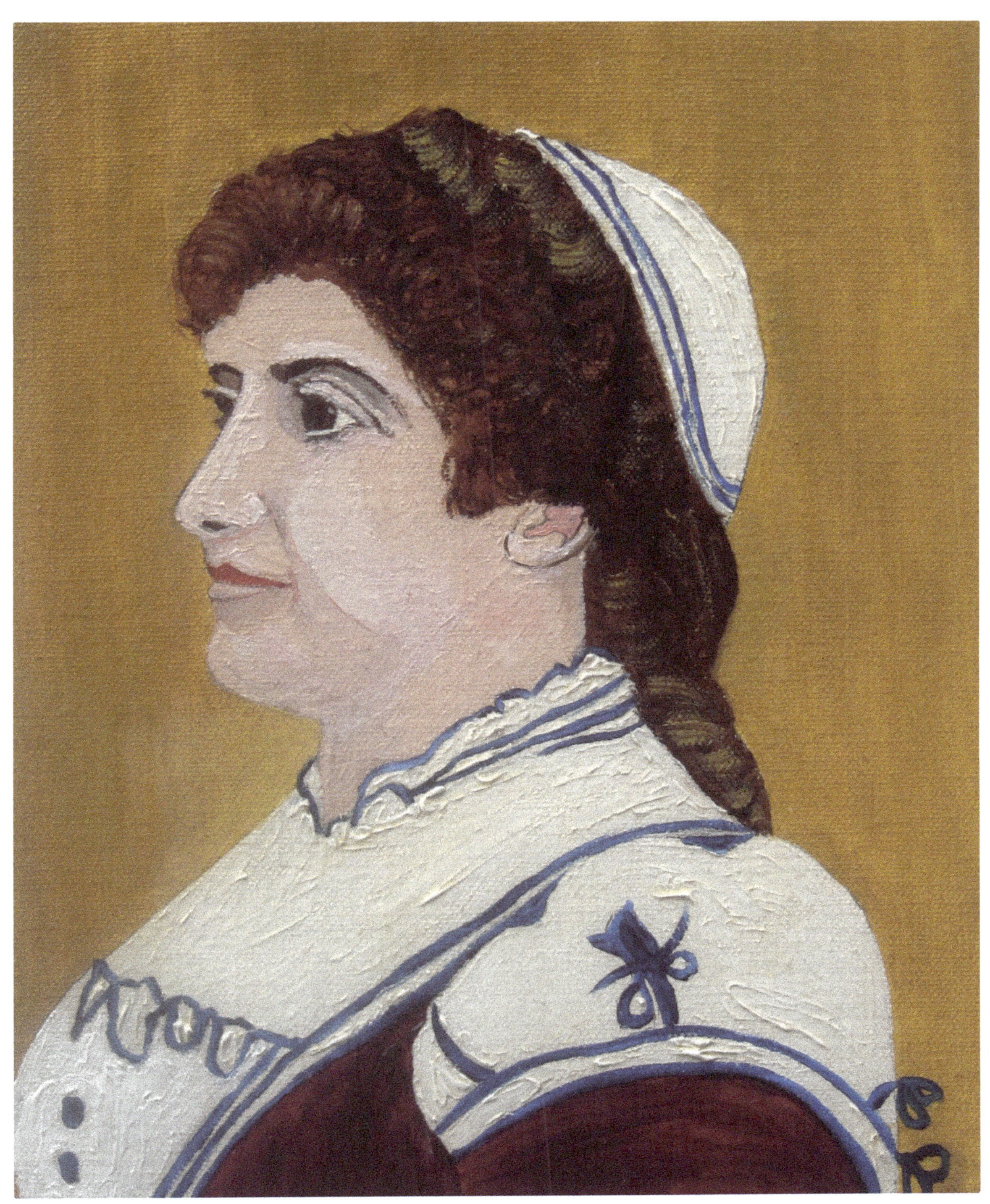

LAURITZ MELCHIOR
Heldentenor

Born in Copenhagen, Denmark, in 1890; died in Santa Monica, California, 1973. Debuts: Copenhagen, 1913, as a baritone in the role of Silvio, (*Pagliacci*); Covent Garden, 1924, as Siegmund (*Die Walkuere*); the Met, 1926 as Tannhaeuser (*Tannhaeuser*). His Covent Garden appearances led to an invitation from Cosima and Siegfried Wagner to sing Parsifal that year, 1924, at Bayreuth. He was the outstanding heldentenor of his time.

Lauritz Melchior as Tristan
(*Tristan und Isolde*)

Tristan und Isolde, opera in 3 acts by **Richard Wagner**, first performed in Munich, Hoftheater, 1865.

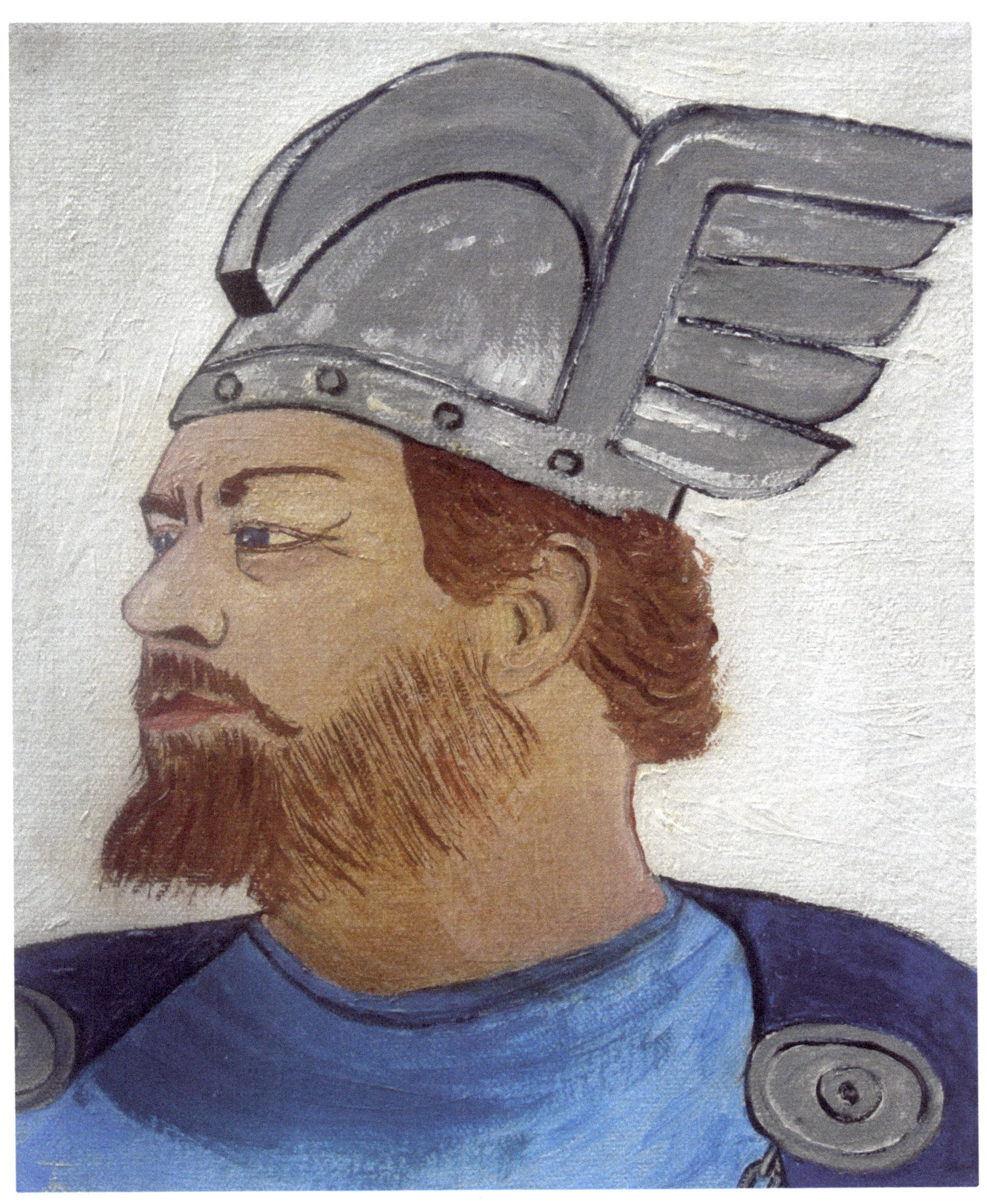

ROBERT MERRILL
Baritone

Born in Brooklyn, N.Y., 1917, died in New York, N.Y., 2004.
After winning the Met Auditions of the Air, he made his Met debut
in 1945 as Germont, a role he sang at the Met 85 times in 30 seasons.
The best American lyric baritone of his generation, Merrill performed
primarily with the Met but was internationally acclaimed, in part
because of his many superlative recordings. He made debuts in
San Francisco (1957), Chicago (1960), La Fenice,
Venice (1961) and Covent Garden (1967).

Robert Merrill as Germont
(*La Traviata*)

La Traviata, opera in 3 acts by **Giuseppe Verdi**,
first performed at La Fenice, Venice, 1853.

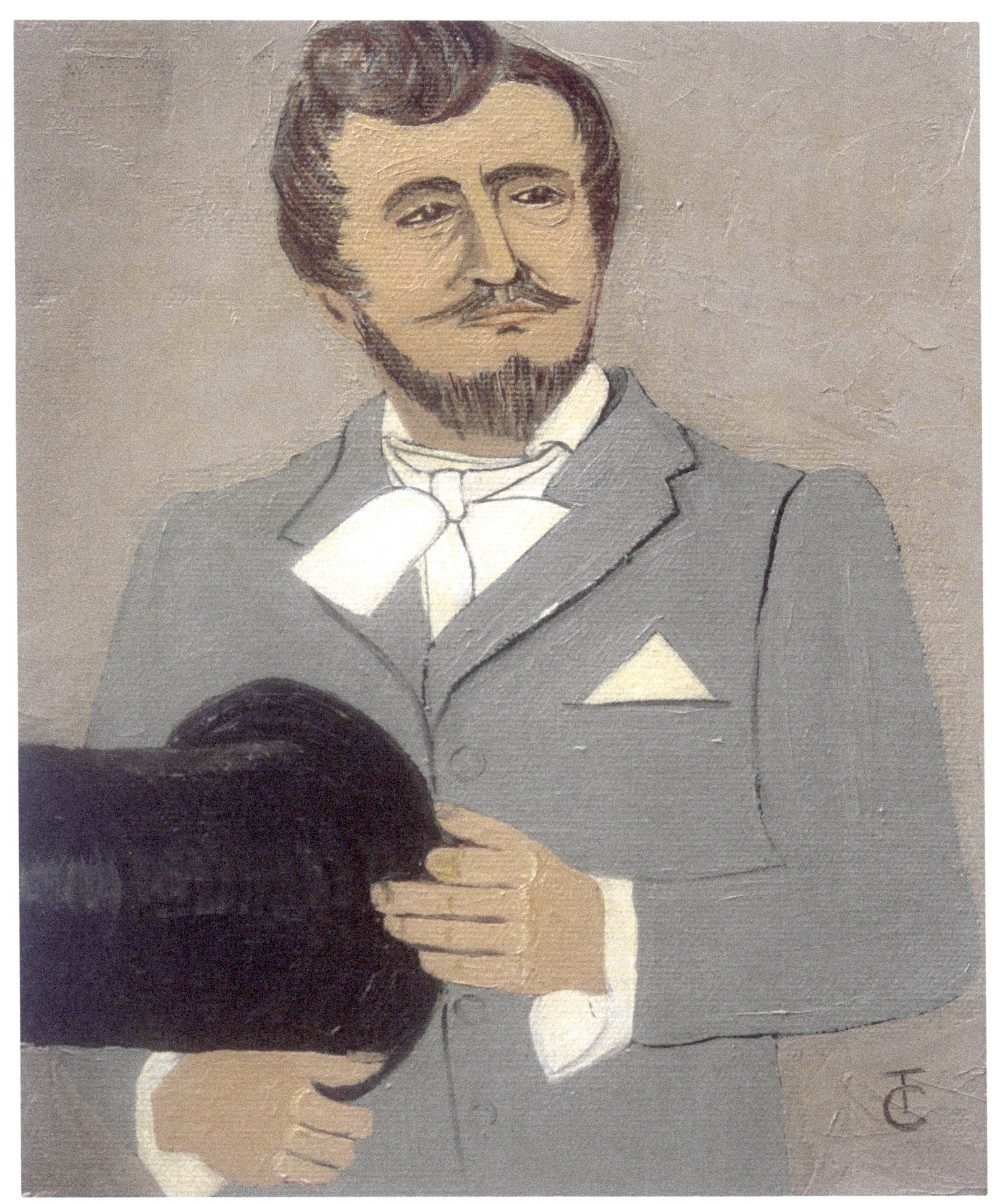

ZINKA MILANOV
Soprano

Born in Zagreb, Croatia, 1906, died in New York, N.Y., 1989. Debut as Leonora (*Il Trovatore*), Ljubljana, 1927. Sang leading roles at Zagreb Opera 1928-35. Sang the Verdi Requiem under Toscanini at Salzburg in 1937 and made her Met debut as Leonora the same year. Other debuts: Chicago, 1940, as Aida; San Francisco, 1943, as Leonora (*La forza del destino*); La Scala, 1950, as Tosca; and Covent Garden, 1956, as Tosca. During 24 seasons at the Met, she sang 298 performances of 13 roles in the Italian dramatic repertory.

Zinka Milanov as Amelia
(*Un ballo in maschera*)

Un ballo in maschera, opera in 3 acts by **Giuseppi Verdi**,
first performed in Rome, 1859.

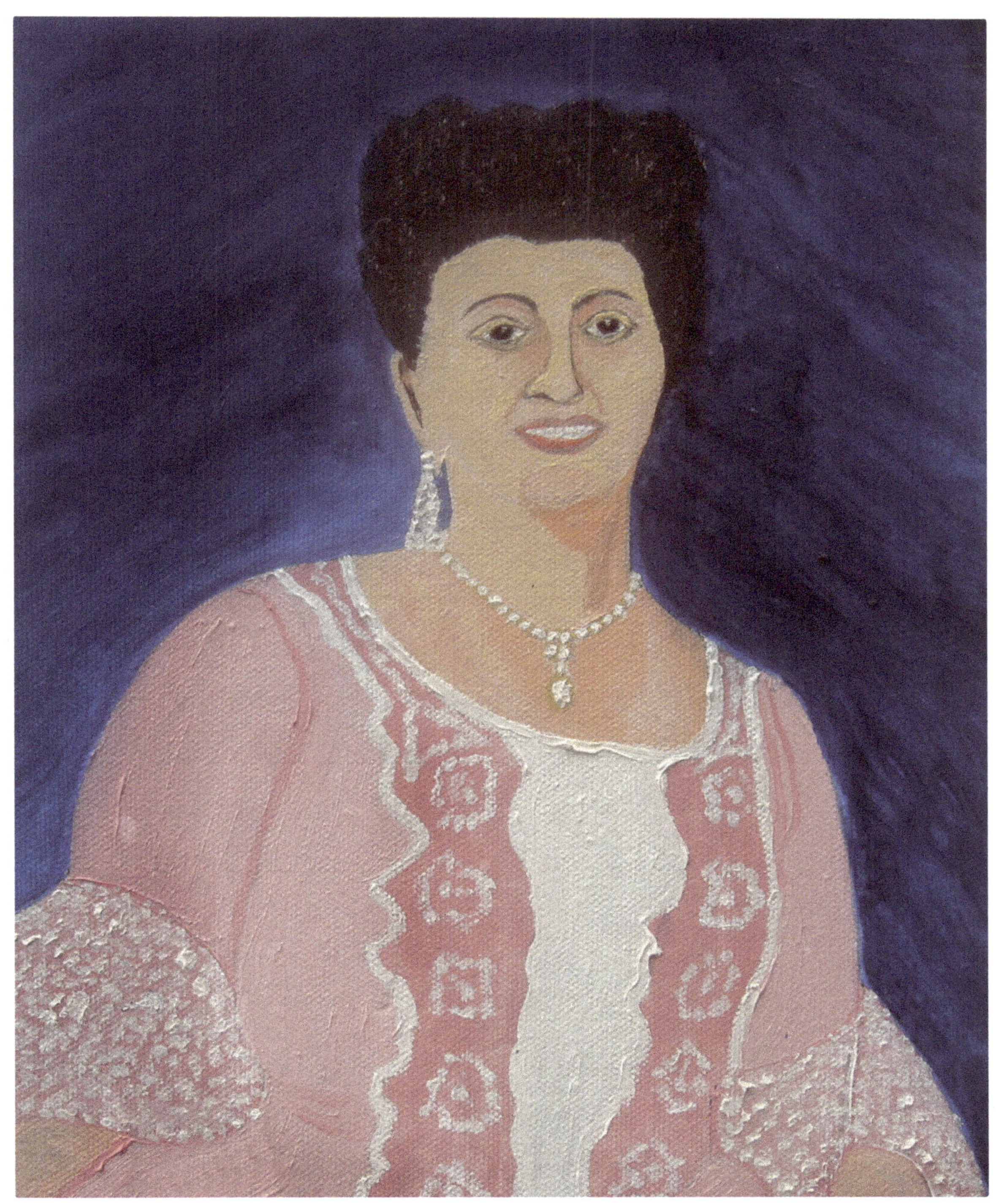

SHERRILL MILNES
Baritone

———————◆———————

Born in Downers Grove, Illinois, 1935. Began his career
with the Opera Company of Boston in 1960 and made his first major
debut as Valentin in Gounod's *Faust* with New York City Opera in
1964. The same year he made his European debut as Figaro in *The
Barber of Seville* in the Teatro Nuovo in Milan. In 1965 he made his
Metropolitan Opera debut as Valentin and returned to the Met
every year through 1988 singing more than 375 performances of 30
roles. Generally considered the pre-eminent baritone of the latter
half of the 20th century, he is particularly celebrated as the
master of Verdi roles. He is one of the major and most
prolific recording artists of his generation.

Sherrill Milnes as Rigoletto
(*Rigoletto*)

Rigoletto, opera in 3 acts by **Giuseppe Verdi**,
first performed in Venice, La Fenice, 1851.

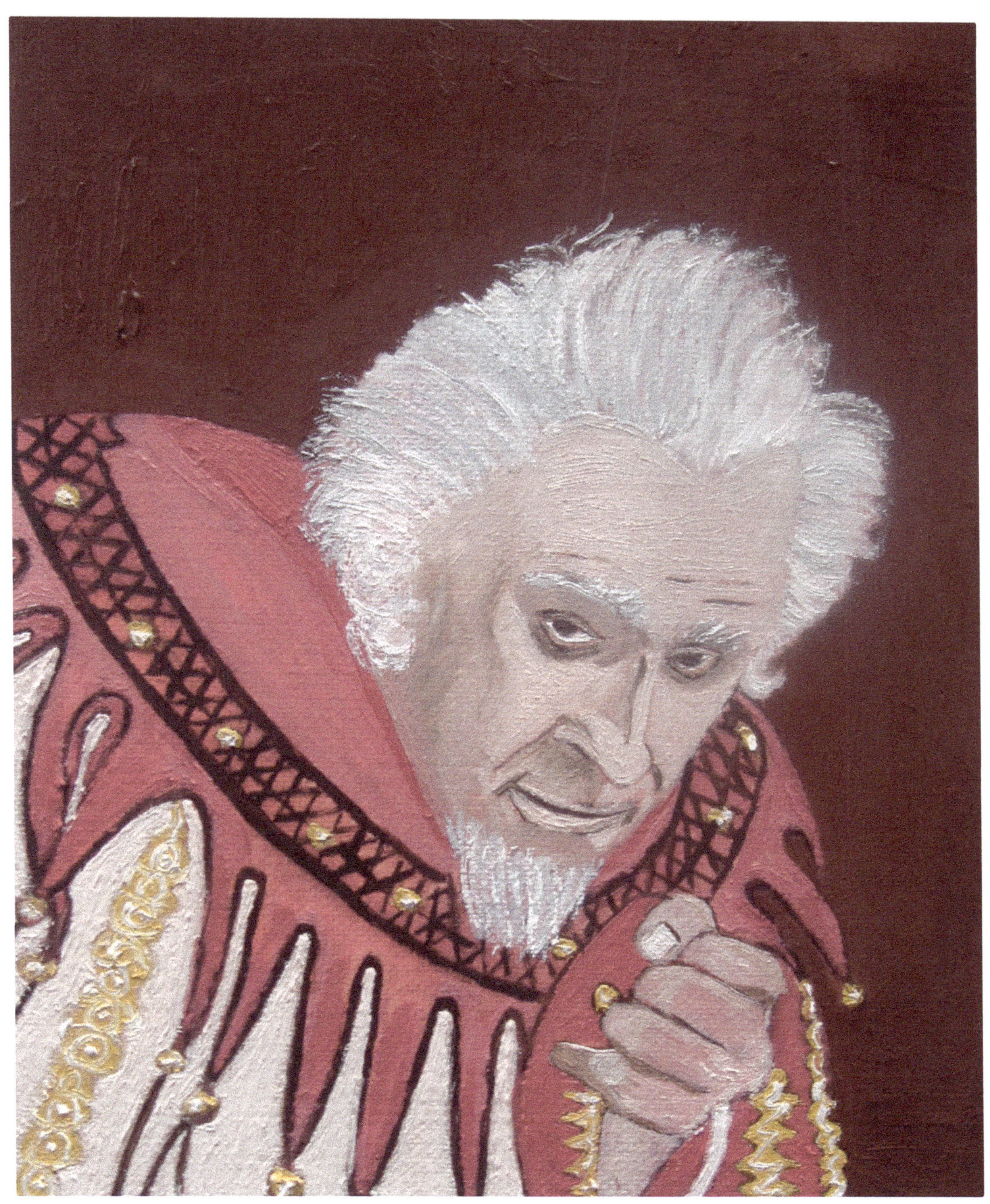

BIRGIT NILSSON
Dramatic Soprano

Born in West Karup, Sweden, 1918; died in Bjardov, Sweden, 2005.
Debuts: Stockholm, 1946, as Agatha (*Der Freischutz*); Glyndebourne,
1951, as Electra (*Idomeneo*). Her early international performances in
Wagner operas were at Bayreuth (Elsa, 1954; Isolde, 1957); Covent
Garden (Bruennhilde, 1957); and the Met (Isolde, 1958). The finest
Wagnerian soprano of the post-war period, Nilsson was also
much admired in her roles as Puccini's Tosca and Turandot,
and Strauss's Salome and Electra.

Birgit Nilsson as Turandot
(*Turandot*)

Turandot, opera in 3 acts by **Giacomo Puccini**,
first performed in Milan at La Scala, 1926.

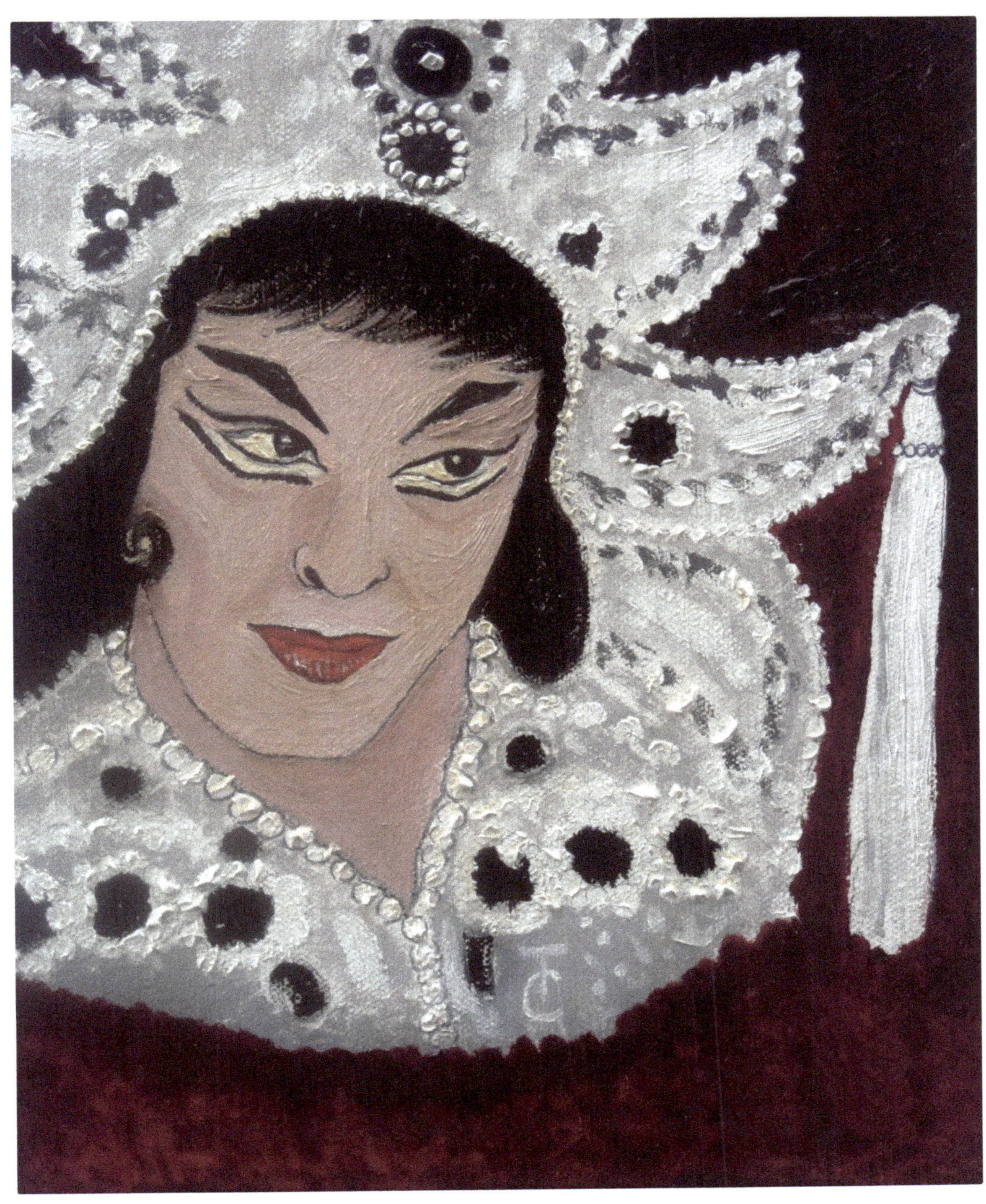

A D E L I N A   P A T T I
Soprano

Born in Madrid, Spain, 1843; died in Brecon, Wales, 1919. Debut as Lucia at the Academy of Music, New York, 1859. Succeeding debuts were in London as Amina (*La Sonnambula*), Berlin (1861), Brussels and Paris (1862), Vienna (1863), Italy (1865) and Russia (1867). She appeared at La Scala 1877-78, Paris Opera, 1874 and 1888, and in the Met's initial seasons 1883-85. "The reign of Patti" lasted almost half a century, during most of which time her mastery of coloratura was reportedly unrivalled.

Adelina Patti as Marguerite
(*Faust*)

Faust, opera in 5 acts by **Charles Gounod**,
first performed at Paris, Theatre-Lyrique, 1859.

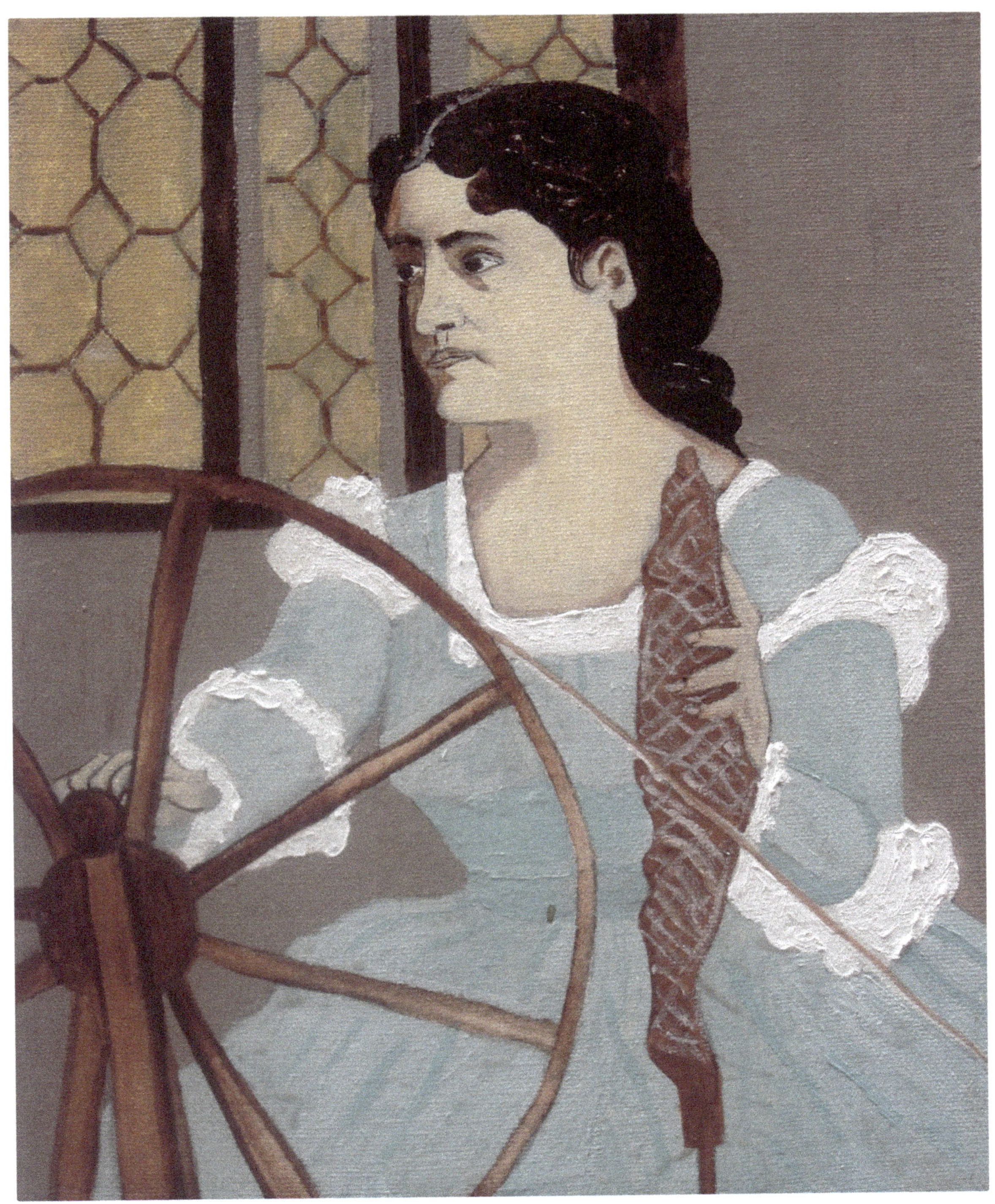

LUCIANO PAVAROTTI
Tenor

Born in Modena, Italy, 1935; died in Modena, Italy, 2007.
Debut as Rodolfo (*La Bohème*) in Reggio Emilia (1961), Vienna (1963), Covent Garden (1963), Naples (1964), La Scala (1965), San Francisco (1967), the Met (1968), and Chicago (1973). He sang opposite Joan Sutherland in 1965-66 at Covent Garden and on tour in Australia in operas by Bellini, Donizetti and Verdi. His sweet, bright lyric tenor, charming stage presence and remarkable recording and television celebrity combined to make him probably the best known and admired tenor since Enrico Caruso.

Luciano Pavarotti was a king among tenors.

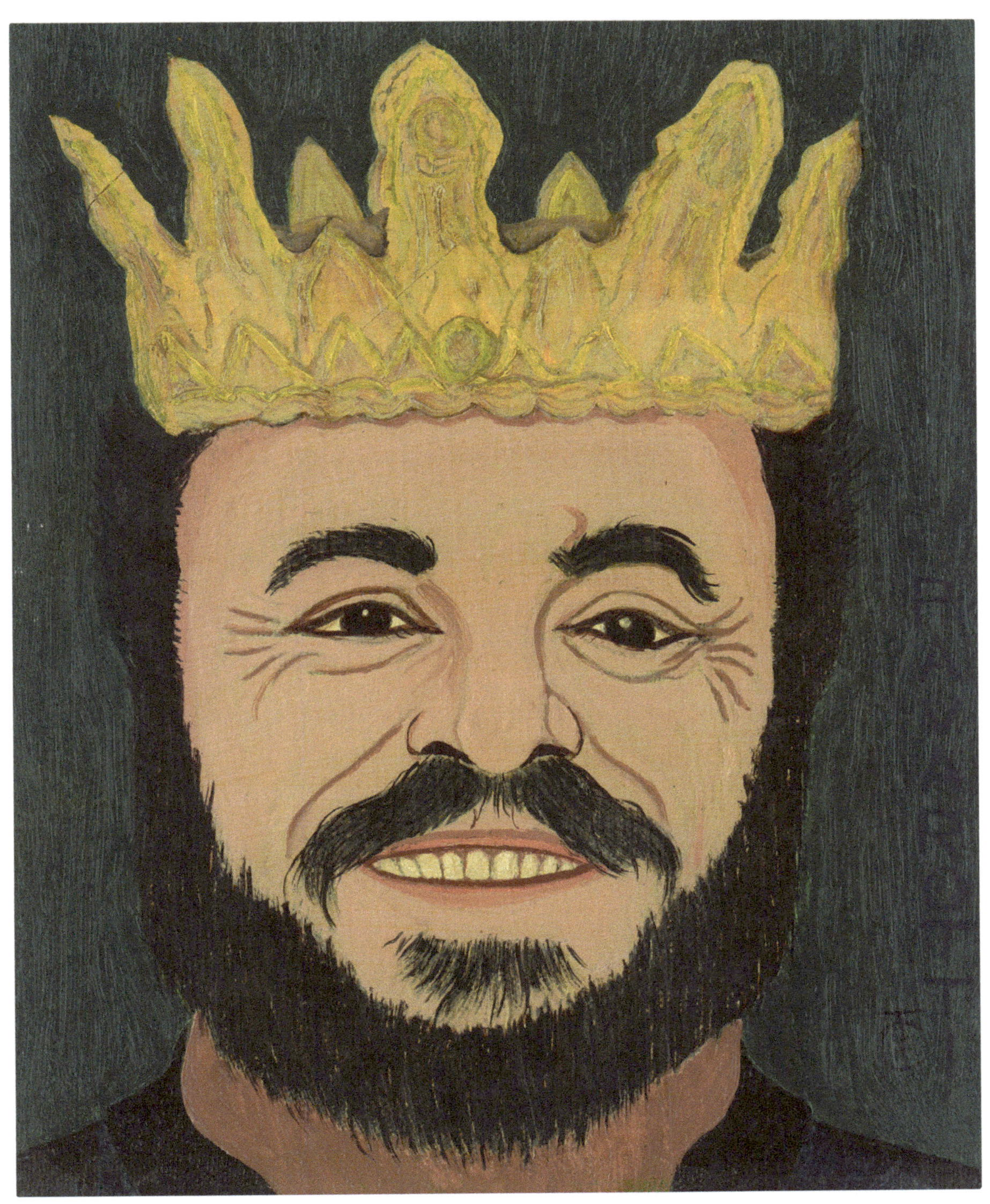

EZIO PINZA
Bass

Born in Rome, Italy, 1892; died in Stamford, Connecticut, 1957.
Debuts: Cremona, 1914, as Oroveso (*Norma*); Rome, 1919; La Scala,
1922, as Pimen (*Boris Godunov*); the Met, 1926 in *La Vestale*; San
Francisco, 1927, as Timur (*Turandot*). He sang regularly at the Met
and San Francisco until 1948. His Don Giovanni, Mephistopheles and
Boris were universally celebrated. The pre-eminent Italian bass of his
day, he also had a large repertoire of over 95 roles that included French,
German and Russian operas. He began a second career in musical
comedy when he attracted a huge new audience for his singing
in "South Pacific" in 1949.

Ezio Pinza as Don Giovanni
(*Don Giovanni*)

Don Giovanni, opera in 2 acts by **Wolfgang Amadeus Mozart**,
first performed in Prague, Tyl Theatre, 1787.

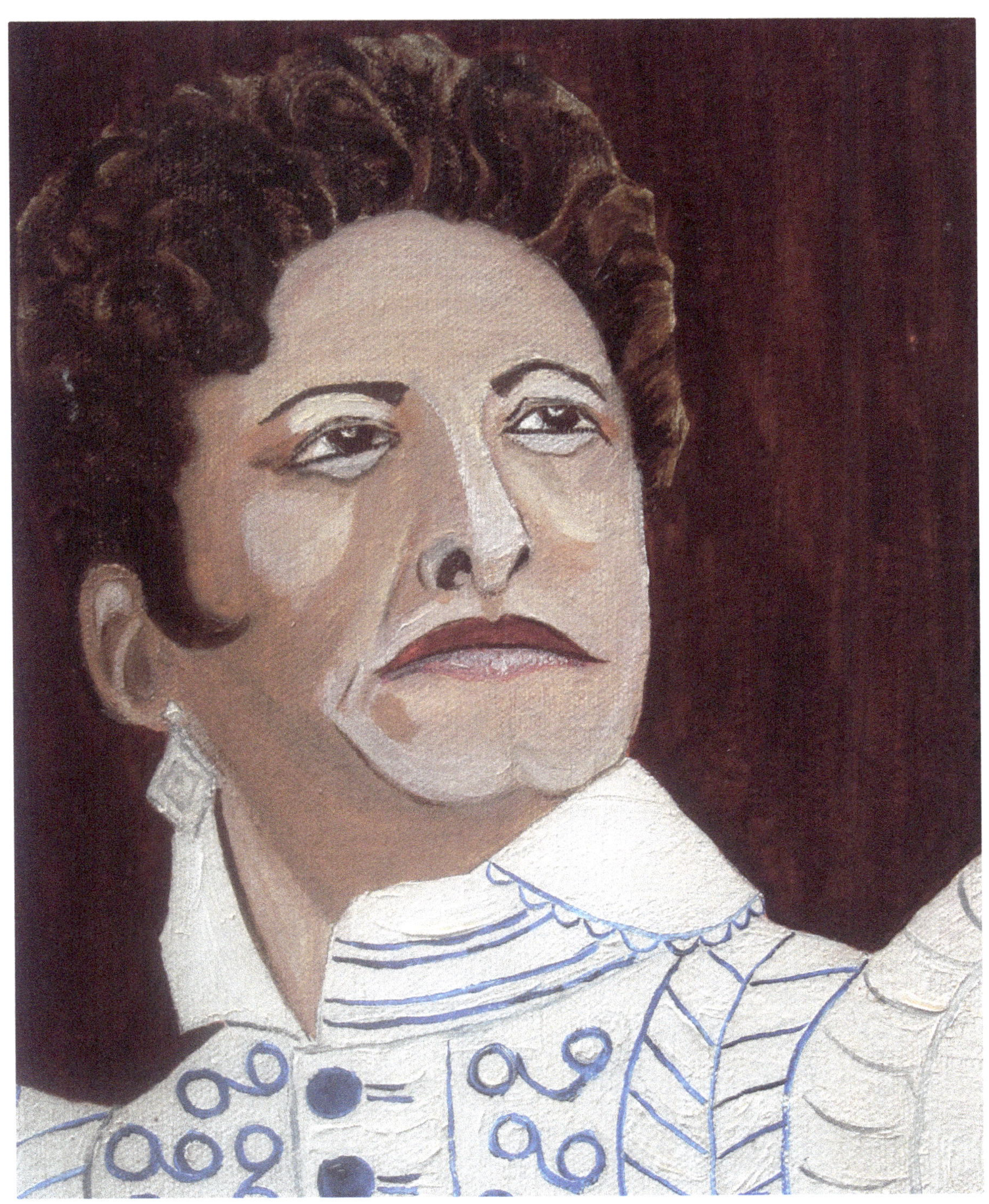

LILY PONS
Coloratura Soprano

Born in Draguignan, France, 1898; died in Dallas, Texas, 1976.
Debut: Mulhouse, France, 1928, as Lakmé, which became her most
famous role. She had a sensational debut at the Met as Lucia (*Lucia di
Lammermoor*) in 1931, with Gigli, de Luca and Pinza. She remained
at the Met for 28 years. She sang regularly in San Francisco
from 1932 to 1951 and in Chicago from 1936 to 1941. Her
remarkably sweet voice and theatrical glamor made
her a popular favorite on radio, in the movies
and on the opera stage.

Lily Pons as Lakmé
(*Lakmé*)

Lakmé, opera in 3 acts by **Leo Delibes**,
first performed in Paris, Opera Comique, in 1883.

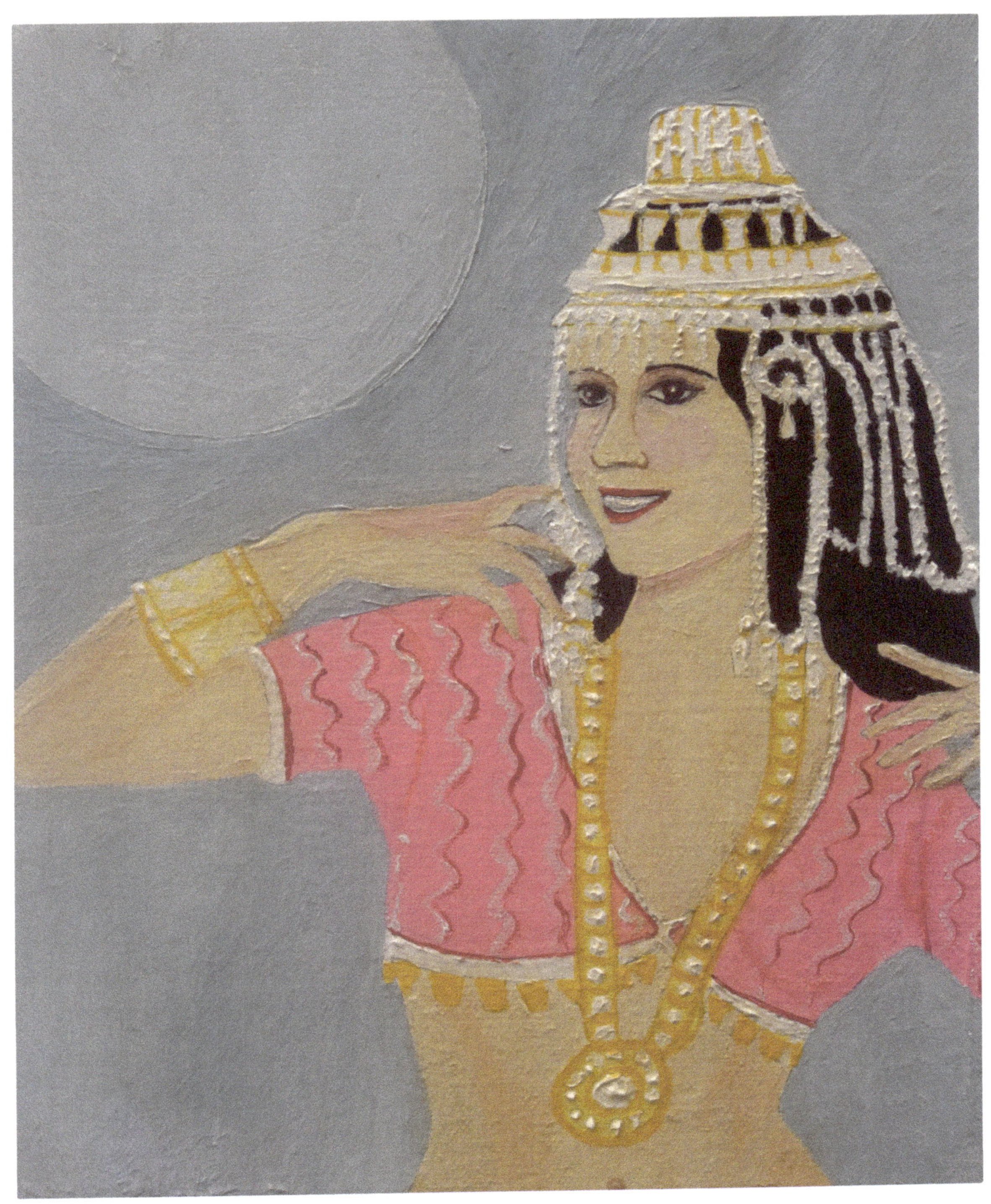

ROSA PONSELLE
Soprano

Born in Meriden, Connecticut, 1897; died in Baltimore,
Maryland, 1981. Debuts: the Met 1918, as Leonora in
the company's first production of *La forza del destino*,
singing opposite Caruso; and Covent Garden, 1929, as
Norma. She sang the mezzo role of Amneris (*Aida*) at
the Met in 1925. Her voice, described by Tullio Serafin
as "a miracle," was one of the most remarkable of
the century, as may be heard on the many
recordings she made.

Rosa Ponselle as Norma
(*Norma*)

Norma, opera in 2 acts by **Vincenzo Bellini**,
first performed in Milan, Teatro alla Scala, 1831.

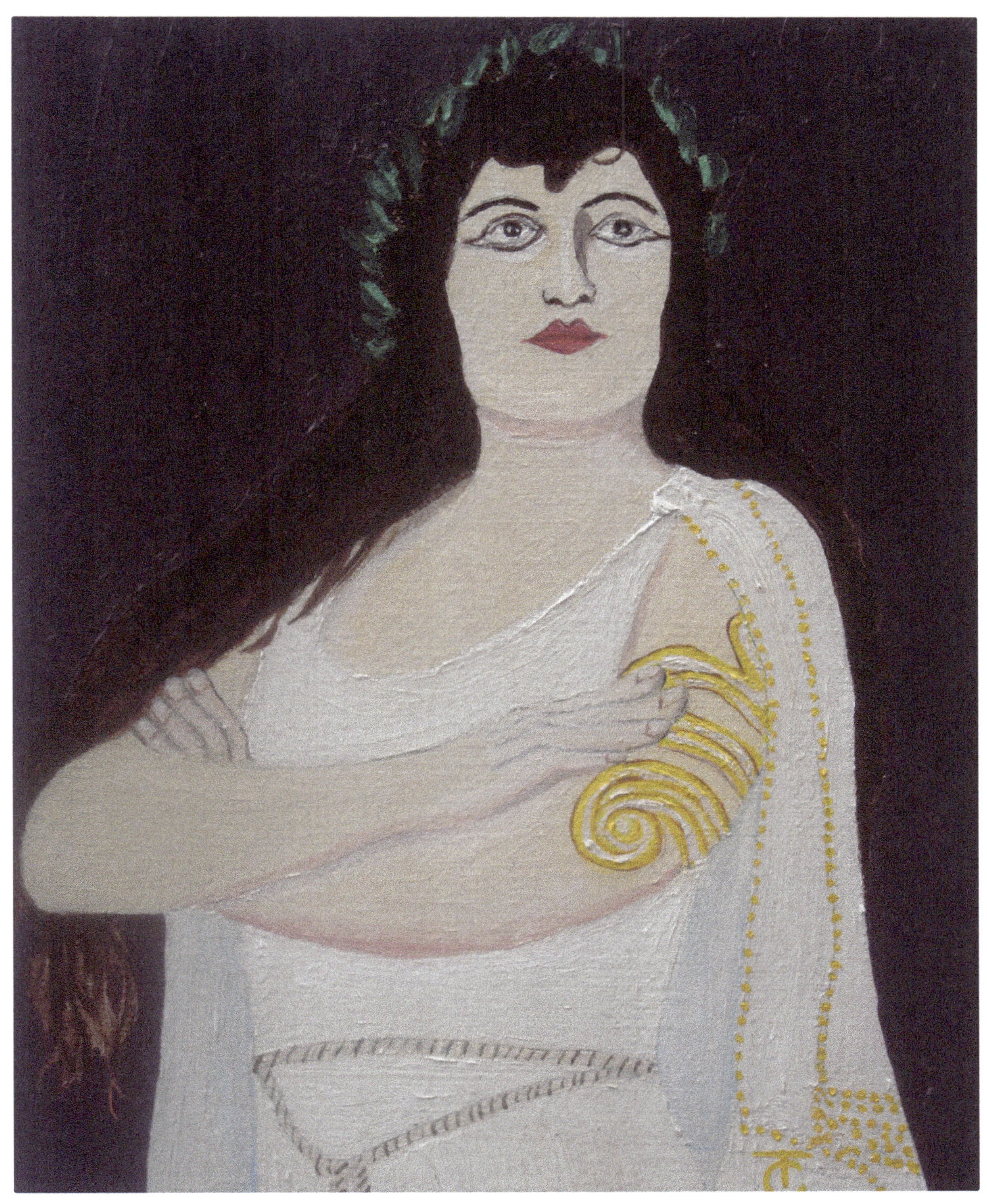

LEONTYNE PRICE
Soprano

Born in Laurel, Mississippi, 1927. Debuts: San Francisco,
1957, as Mme. Lidione in the U.S. premier of *Les Dialogues
des Carmelites* (Poulenc), followed by her first Aida in Verona;
Vienna (under Karajan) and Covent Garden, in 1958; La Scala,
1960, as Aida; and the Met, 1961, as Leonora in *Il Trovatore*.
Her rich, expressive voice was ideally suited to the great
dramatic soprano roles that she favored, including
Aida, Leonora, Carmen and Tosca.

Leontyne Price as Aida
(*Aida*)

Aida, opera in 4 acts by **Giuseppe Verdi**,
first performed in Cairo, Egypt, 1871.

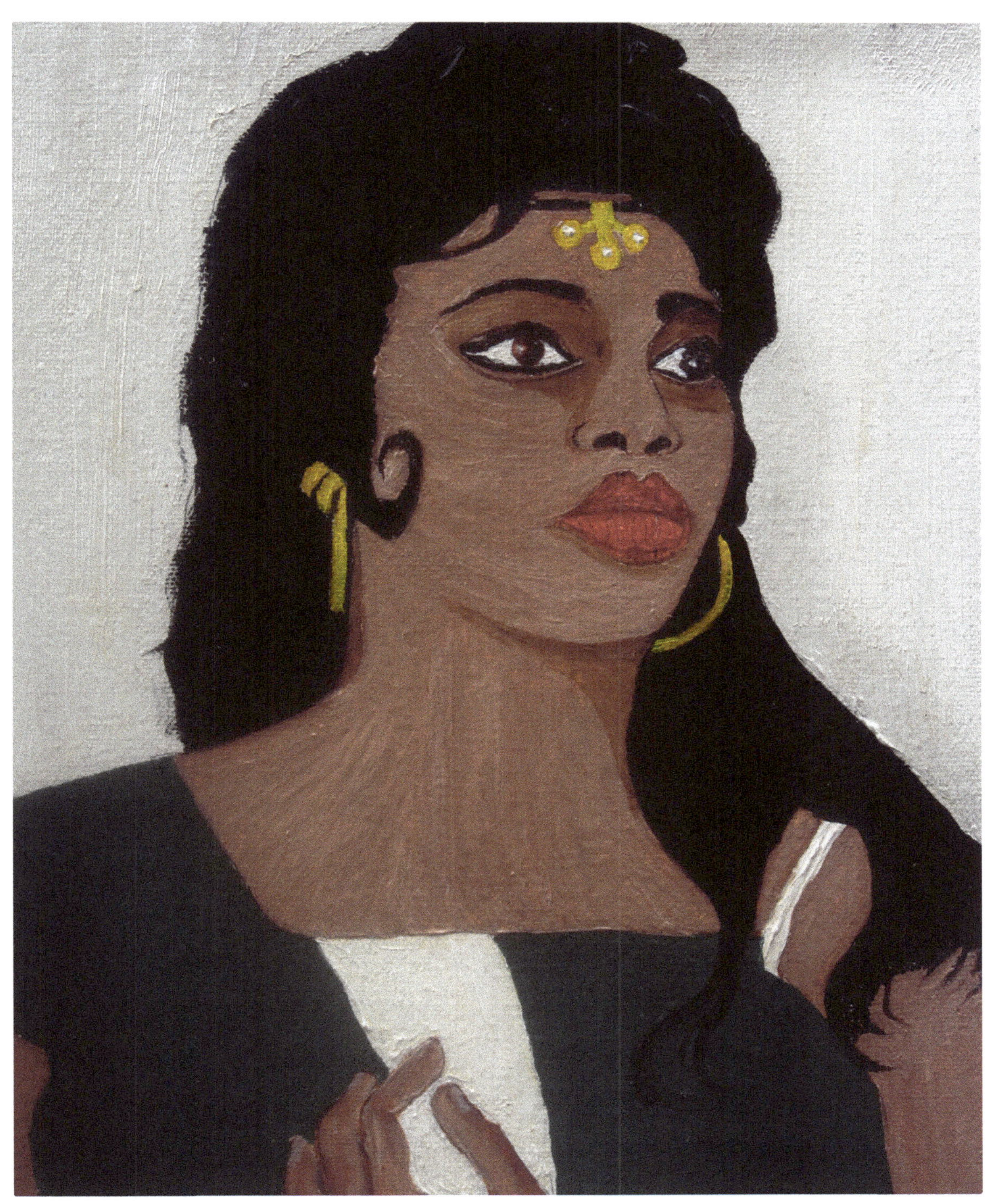

TITTA RUFFO
Baritone

Born in Pisa, Italy, 1877; died in Florence, Italy, 1953.
Debuts: Costanzi, Rome as the Herald (*Lohengrin*), 1898;
Covent Garden, 1903; La Scala as Rigoletto (*Rigoletto*), 1904;
Teatro Colon, Buenos Aires, 1908; Paris, 1911; Philadelphia,
1912; and the Met, 1922, as Figaro (*Il Barbiere di Siviglia*), his
most frequently performed role in his 8 seasons at the
Met. Endowed with the most imposing baritone
voice of his generation, Ruffo, reputedly, had
an aggressive, dramatic style on stage.

Titta Ruffo as Figaro
(*Il Barbiere di Siviglia*)

Il Barbiere di Siviglia, opera buffo in 2 acts by **Gioacchino Rossini**,
first performed in Rome, Teatro Argentina, 1816.

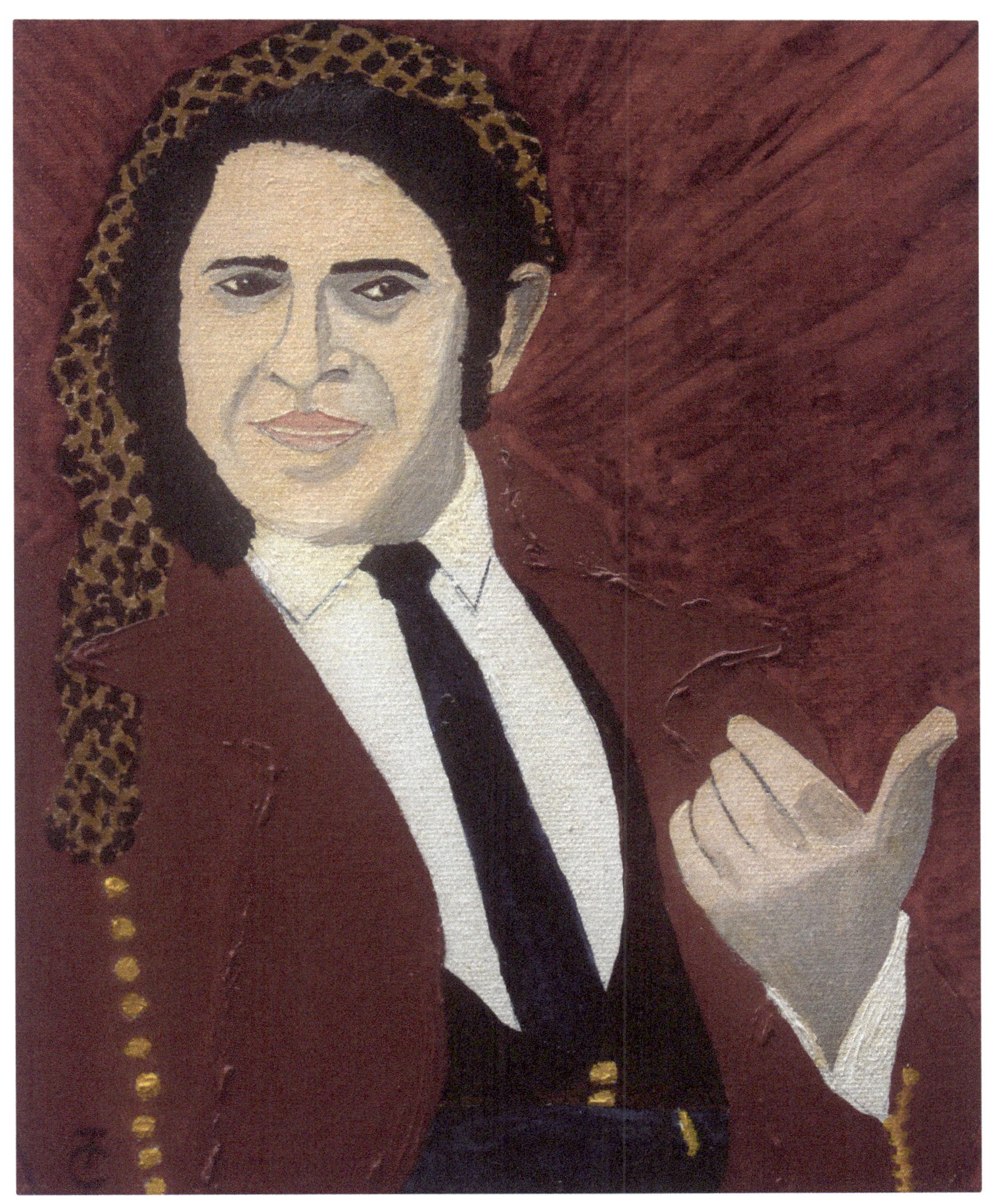

ELISABETH SCHWARZKOPF
Soprano

Born in Jarocin, Poland, 1915; died in Schruns, Austria, 2006.
Debut: Berlin (1938) as a Flower- maiden (*Parsifal*). In Salzburg
(1947-64) she perfected what became her core repertoire: the
Countess (*Le Nozze di Figaro*), Donna Elvira (*Don Giovanni*), Alice
Ford (*Falstaff*), Fiordiligi (*Così fan tutte*) and the Marschallin (*Der
Rosenkavalier*). At La Scala, she created the role of Anne Trulove in
Stravinsky's *The Rake's Progress*. Her debut in the U.S. was as the
Marschallin at the San Francisco Opera (1955), the role she chose
for her Paris debut in 1962 and her Met debut in 1964.

Elisabeth Schwarzkopf as the Marschallin
(*Der Rosenkavalier*)

Der Rosenkavalier, opera in 3 acts, by **Richard Strauss**,
first performed in Dresden, Germany, 1911.

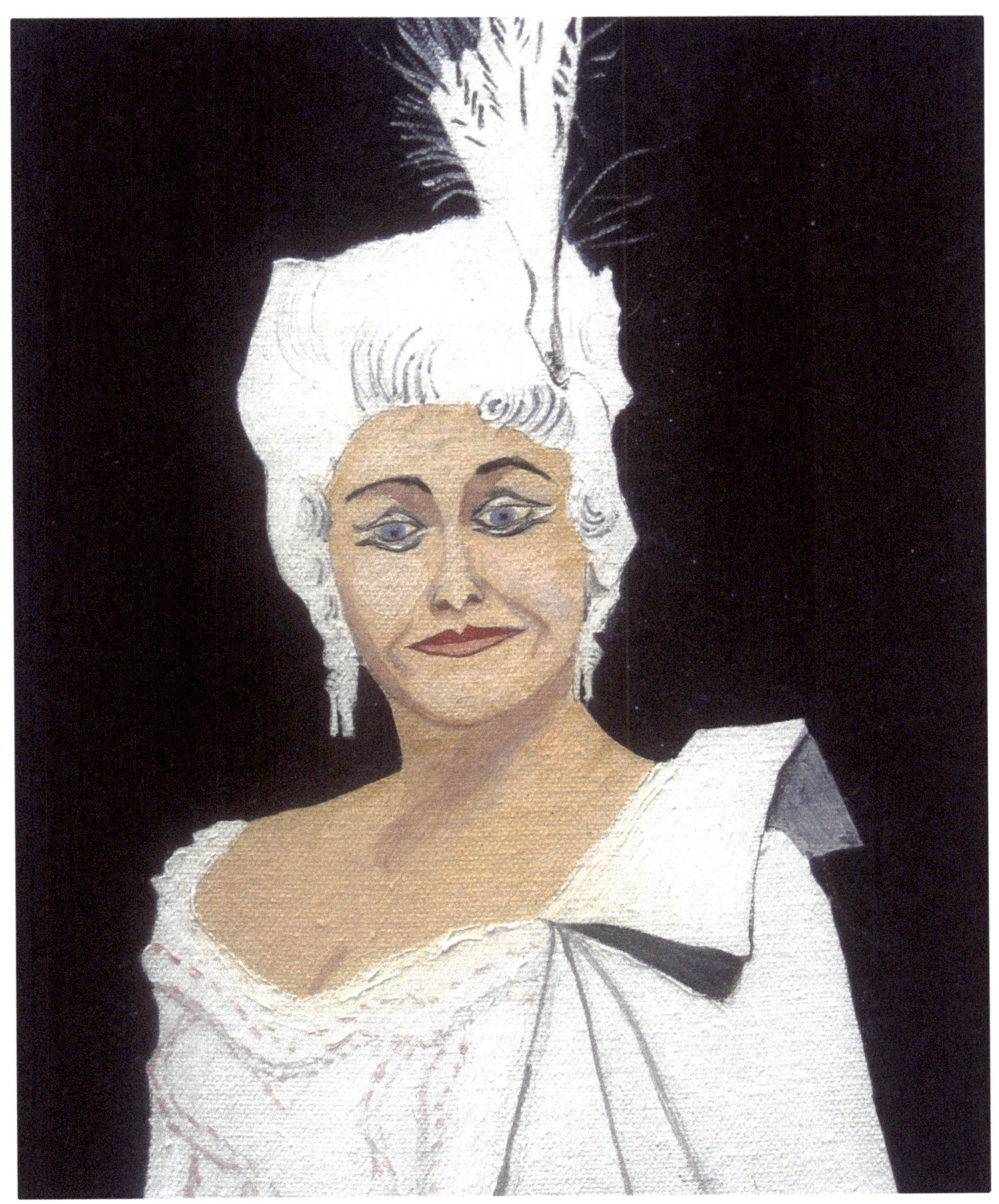

BEVERLY SILLS
Coloratura Soprano

Born in Brooklyn, NY, 1929, died in New York City, 2007.
She made her professional debut in Philadelphia as Frasquita
(*Carmen*), 1946, in San Francisco as Elena (*Mefistofele*), 1953, and at
the Met in 1975 in *Le siège de Corinthe*. For more than two decades
from the 1950s to the 1970s she was the prima donna of New York
City Opera and became that company's general manager in 1965.
Internationally acclaimed for her superb musicianship and as an
actress, she was the chief rival to Joan Sutherland as the
leading bel canto singer of her time.

Beverly Sills as Pamira
(*Le siège de Corinthe*)

Le siège de Corinthe, opera in 3 acts by **Gioacchino Rossini**,
first performed in Paris, Opera, 1826.

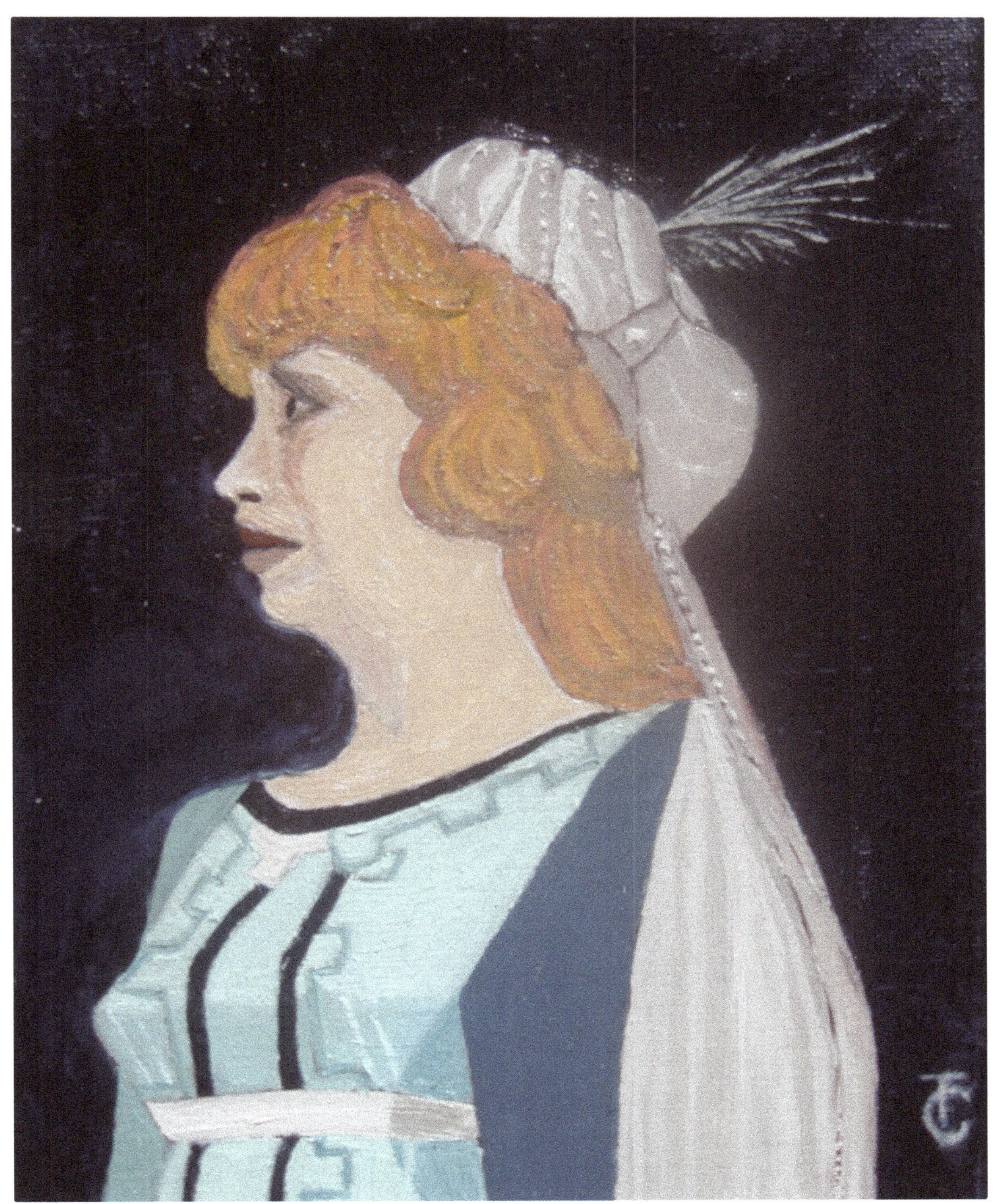

GIULIETTA SIMIONATO
Mezzo

Born in Forli, Italy, in 1910; died in Rome, Italy, 2010.
Debuts: Montagnana, 1928, as Lola (*Cavalleria rusticana*); La
Scala, 1936, as Maddalena (*Rigoletto*); 1953, Covent Garden and
San Francisco; and the Met, 1959, as Rosina (*Il Barbiere di Siviglia*).
Admired equally for the intensity of her performances in tragic roles
and her ebullience in comedy, she was the most versatile Italian
mezzo of her generation.

Giulietta Simionato as Santuzza
(*Cavalleria rusticana*)

Cavalleria rusticana, opera in one act by **Pietro Mascagni**,
first performed in Rome, Teatro Costanzi, 1890.

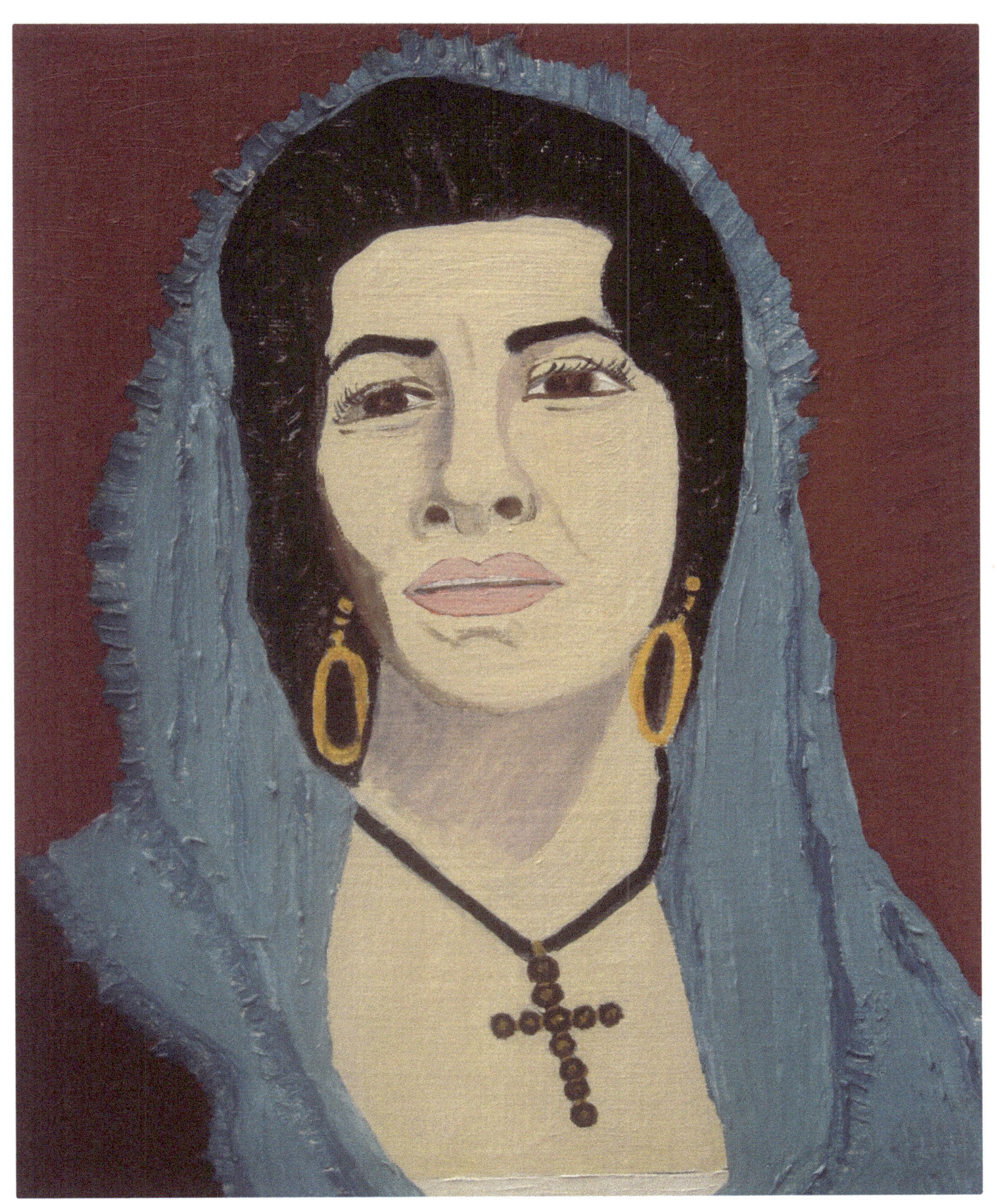

FREDERICA VON STADE
Mezzo

Born in Somerville, NJ, 1945. Professional debut as Third Boy (*Die Zauberfloete*) at the Met, 1970, in Paris and at Glyndebourne, both 1973 and Salzburg, 1974, as Cherubino. Greatly admired for her smooth mezzo, polished technique and refined musicality, her finest roles include Cherubino, and the leads in *Cendrillon*, *Cherubin*, and *Pélléas et Melisande*. She gave her farewell performance on the opera stage in *Dead Man Walking* at Houston Grand Opera in 2011.

Frederica von Stade as Cherubino

(*Le nozze di Figaro*)

Le nozze di Figaro, opera in 4 acts by **Wolfgang Amadeus Mozart**, first performed in Vienna, Burgtheater, 1786.

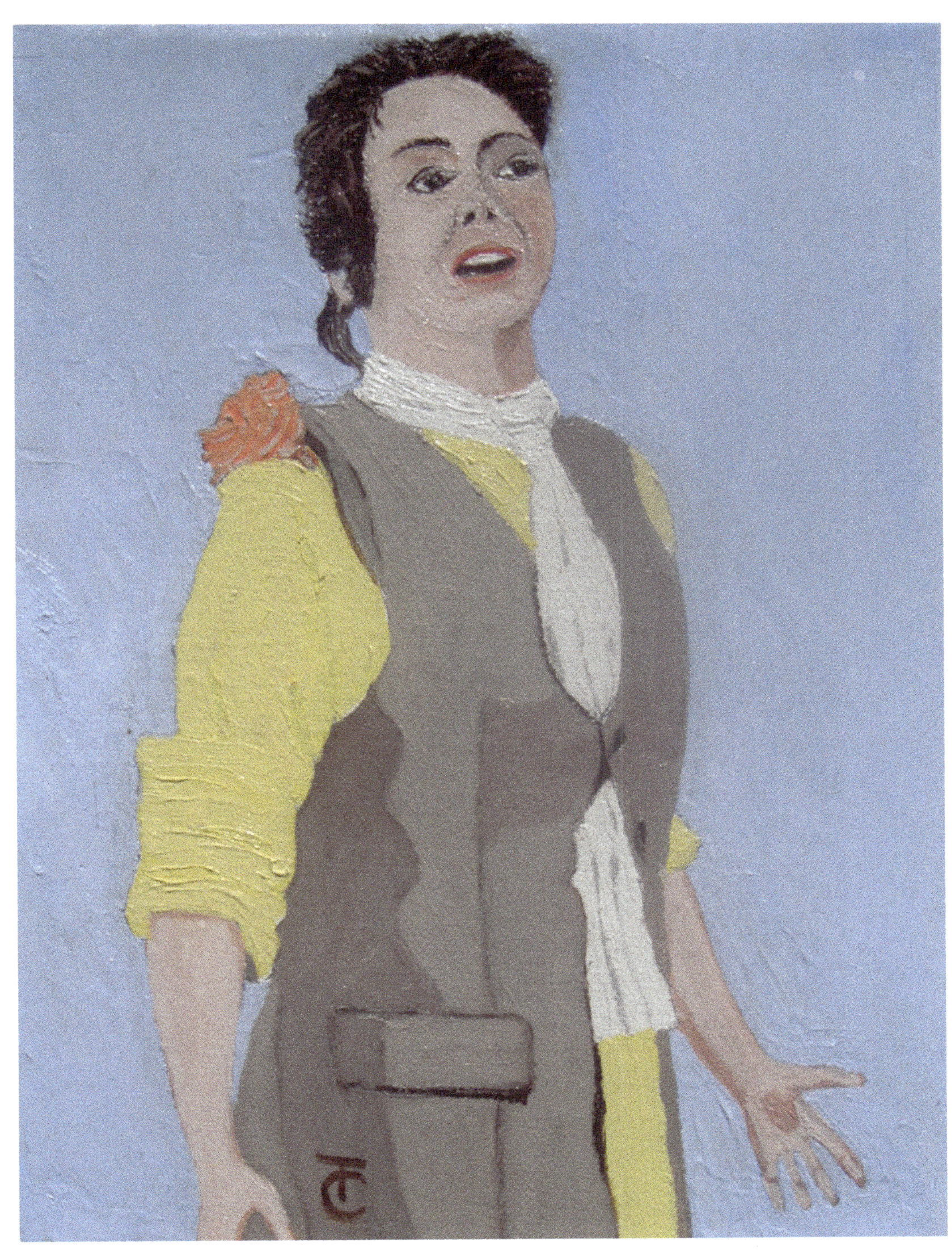

DAME JOAN SUTHERLAND
Soprano

Born in Sydney, Australia, 1926. Debuts: Sydney, 1951, in Goosen's *Judith*; Covent Garden, 1952, as the First Lady (*The Magic Flute*); and as Lucia (*Lucia di Lammermoor*) in Paris, 1960, at La Scala, Chicago and the Met, all in 1961. In 1954 she married the pianist Richard Bonynge, who directed her towards the florid soprano repertory and then in the 1960s became her favored conductor. Her performances, in partnership with Luciano Pavarotti and Marilyn Horne, are captured in several excellent recordings.

Joan Sutherland as Lucia
(*Lucia di Lammermoor*)

Lucia di Lammermoor, opera in 3 acts by **Gaetano Donizetti**, first performed in Naples, Teatro San Carlo, 1835.

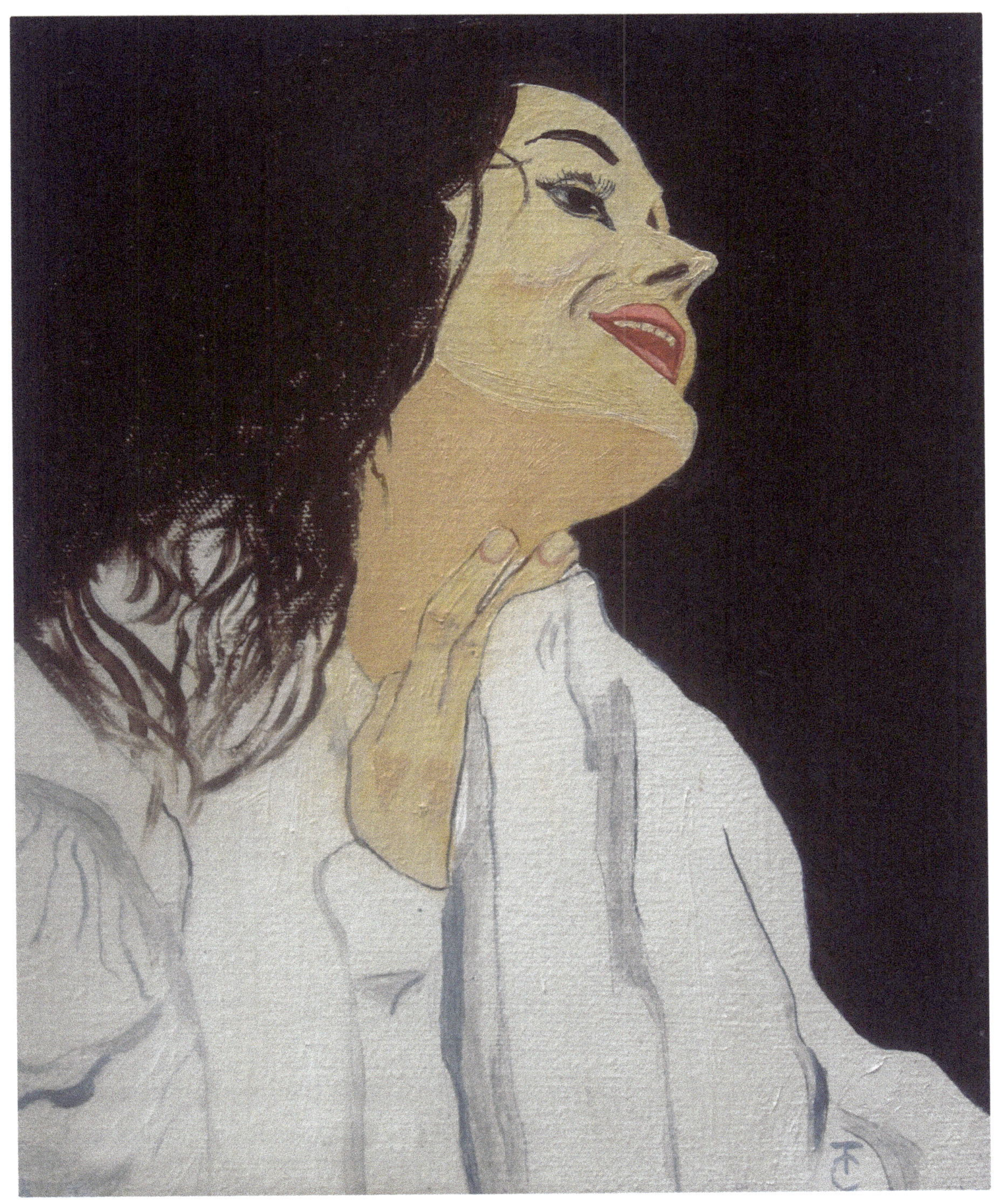

RENATA TEBALDI
Soprano

Born in Pesaro, Italy, 1922; died in San Marino, 2004.

Debut: Rovigo, 1944, as Elena (*Mefistofele*). In 1946 Toscanini chose her to take part in the concert for the reopening of La Scala, and she became the leading soprano of the company. She was first heard outside Italy as Donna Elvira (*Don Giovanni*) in Lisbon, (1949), and then at Covent Garden as Desdemona (*Otello*) in 1950. She made her American debut at San Francisco as Aida (*Aida*) in 1950, and at the Met as Desdemona in 1955. She made her debuts in both Paris and Vienna in 1959. Her glorious voice, preserved in many recordings, was perfectly suited to the Italian repertory.

Renata Tebaldi as Desdemona
(*Otello*)

Otello, opera in 4 acts by **Giuseppe Verdi**,
first performed in Milan, Teatro alla Scala, 1887.

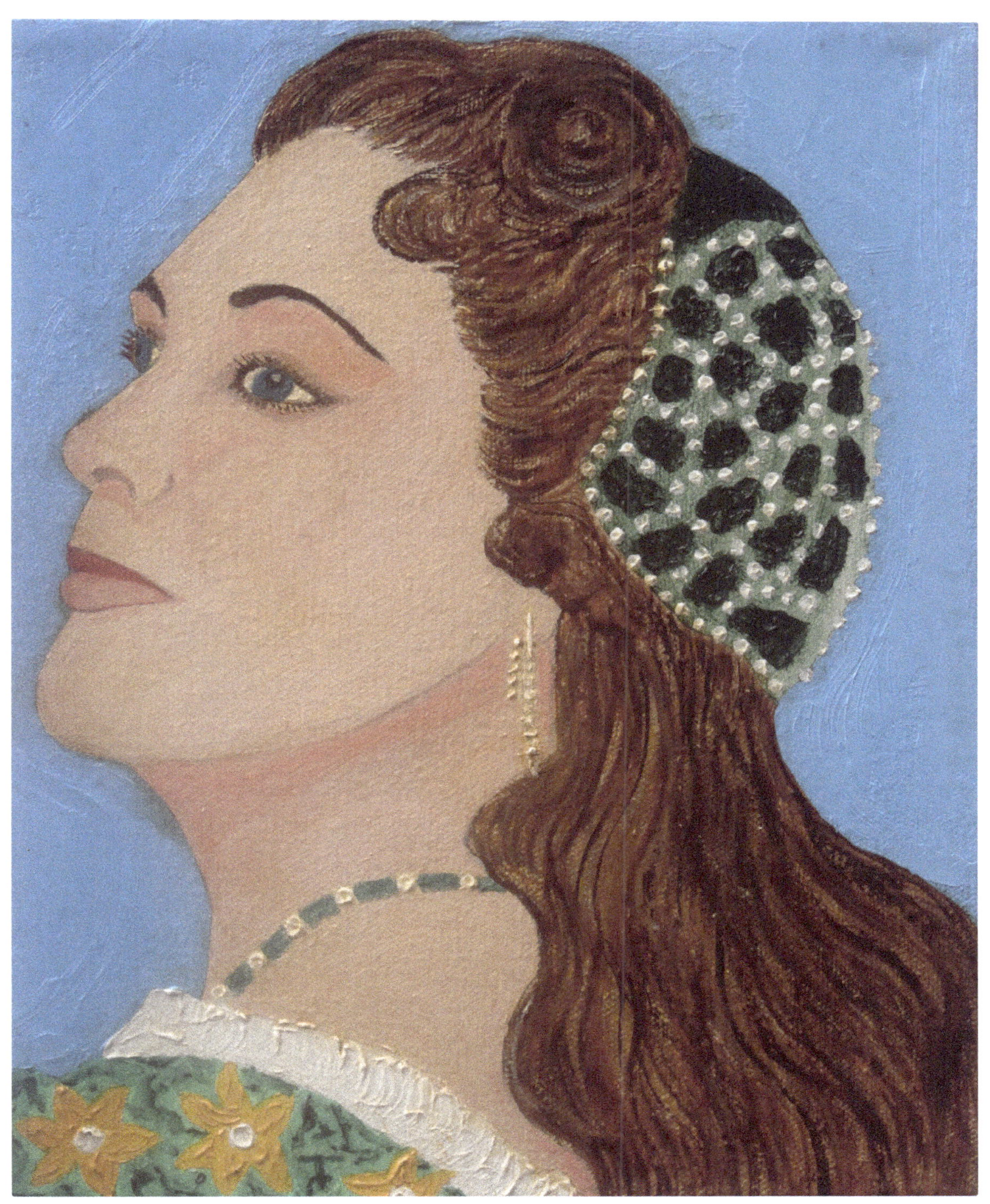

LUISA TETRAZZINI
Coloratura Soprano

Born in Florence, Italy, 1871; died in Milan, Italy, 1940.
Debuts: 1890, Florence, as Ines (*L' Africaine*); South
America, 1893; Spain, 1897. Eastern Europe, 1899;
San Francisco, 1906; Covent Garden, 1907, as Violetta
(*La Traviata*); 1908, New York (Manhatten Opera) as
Violetta. She was a master of coloratura technique,
evidenced by arias and songs recorded
early in her career.

Luisa Tetrazzini as Violetta
(*La Traviata*)

La Traviata, opera in 3 acts by **Giuseppe Verdi**,
first performed at La Fenice, Venice, 1853.

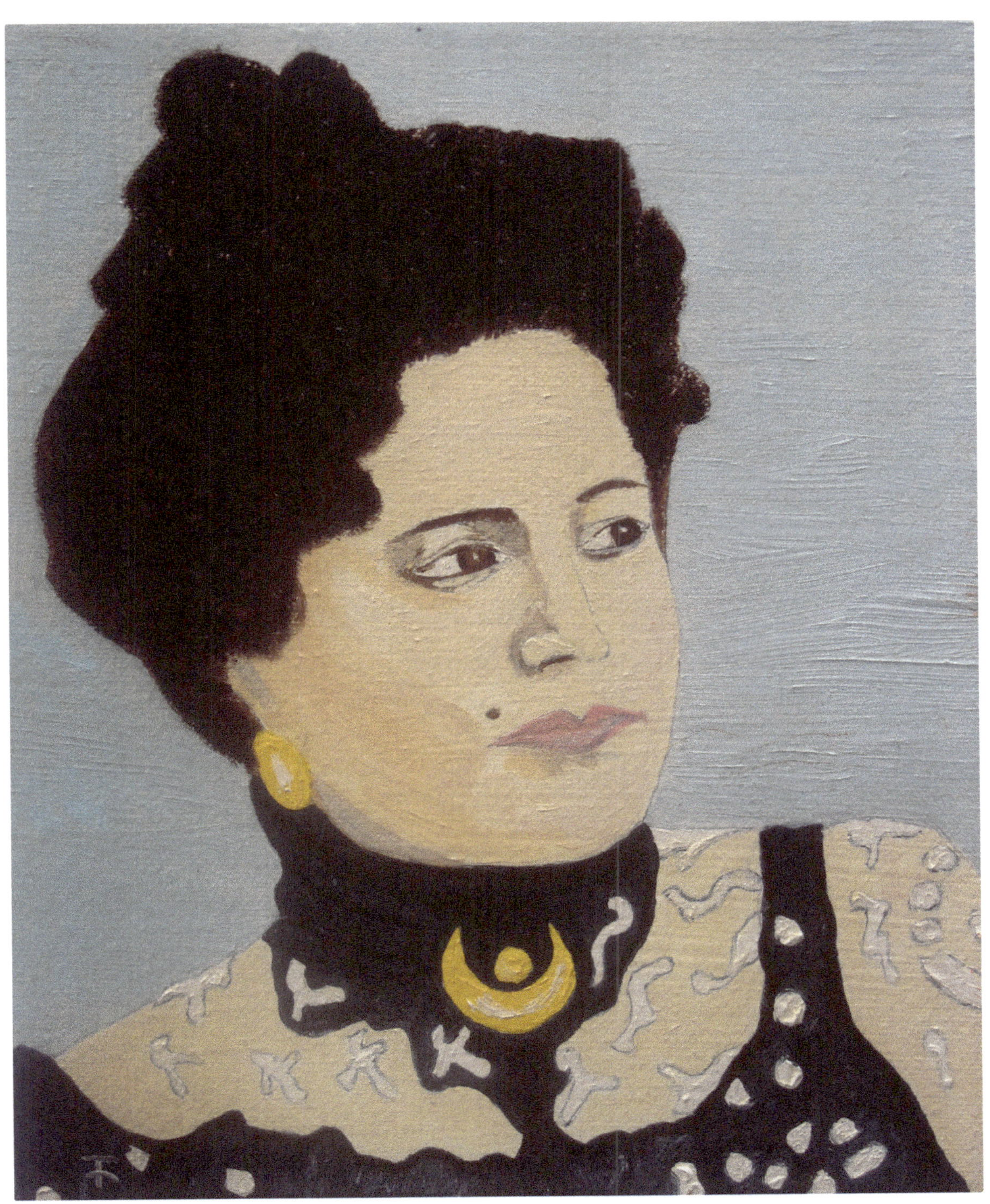

RICHARD TUCKER
Tenor

Born in Brooklyn, N.Y., 1913; died in Kalamazoo, Michigan, 1975.
Debut as Alfredo (*La Traviata*), Salmaggi Opera, Jolson Theater, N.Y.,
1943. Met debut in 1945 as Enzo (Ponchielli's *La Gioconda*), the role in
which he had his Italian debut at the Verona Arena opposite Maria
Callas in her Italian debut. Tucker sang with the Met for 30 seasons
in 499 performances. He was the leading American tenor of his
generation and his distinctive sound is preserved
in many superb recordings.

Richard Tucker as Des Grieux
(*Manon Lescaut*)

Manon Lescaut, opera in 4 acts by **Giacomo Puccini**,
first performed in Turin, Teatro Regio, 1893.

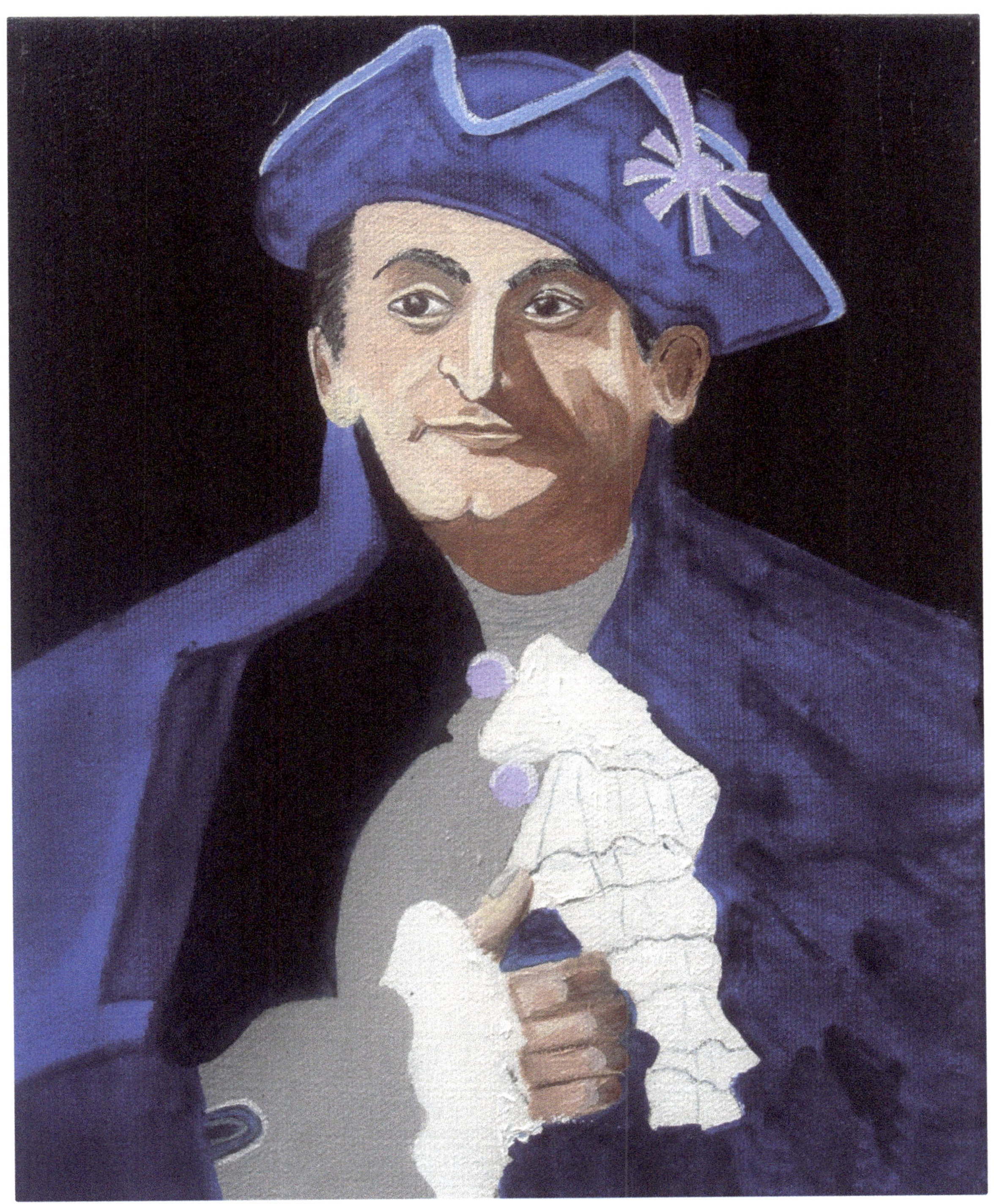

JON VICKERS
Heroic Tenor

Born in Prince Albert, Saskatchewan, Canada, 1926.
Debuts: Toronto, 1952, as the Duke (*Rigoletto*), Covent Garden,
1957; as Riccardo (*Un ballo in maschera*); Bayreuth, as Siegmund
(*Die Walkuere*), 1958; as Canio, (*I Pagliacci*) Vienna, 1959, and the
Met, 1960. One of the great Wagnerian tenors of the age and an
unrivalled Florestan (*Fidelio*) and Peter Grimes (*Peter Grimes*),
he has also been acclaimed in the French repertoire. He had
perhaps the most commanding stage presence of any
male singer of the second half of the 20th century.

Jon Vickers as Peter Grimes
(*Peter Grimes*)

Peter Grimes, opera in a prologue, epilogue and 3 acts
by **Benjamin Britten**, first performed in London, Sadler's
Wells Theatre, 1945.

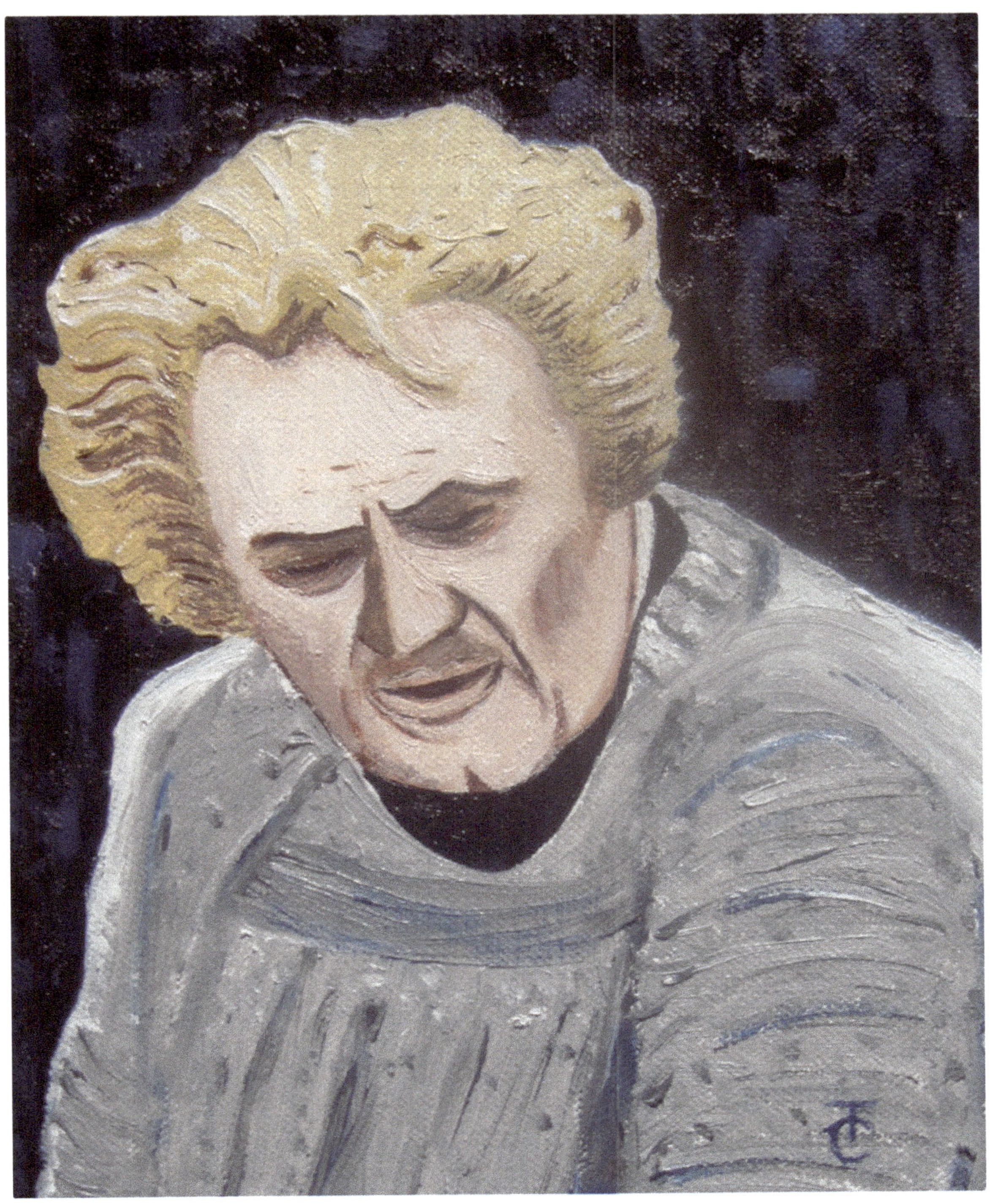

LEONARD WARREN
Baritone

Born in New York, N.Y., 1911; died in New York, N.Y., 1960.
Debuts: the Met, 1939, as Paolo (*Simon Boccanegra*); Rio
de Janeiro, 1942; San Francisco, 1943; and 1953, La Scala,
as Rigoletto (*Rigoletto*). He was the leading Italian baritone
in his 22 seasons with the Met and of the 416 performances
he sang there he is best remembered for his performances as
Rigoletto, 56 times; Amonasro (*Aida*), 37; Iago (*Otello*), 33;
Count di Luna (*Il Trovatore*), 32; and Tonio (*I Pagliacci*), 30.

Leonard Warren as Macbeth
(*Macbeth*)

Macbeth, opera in 4 acts by **Giuseppe Verdi**,
first performed in Florence, Teatro alla Pergola, 1847.

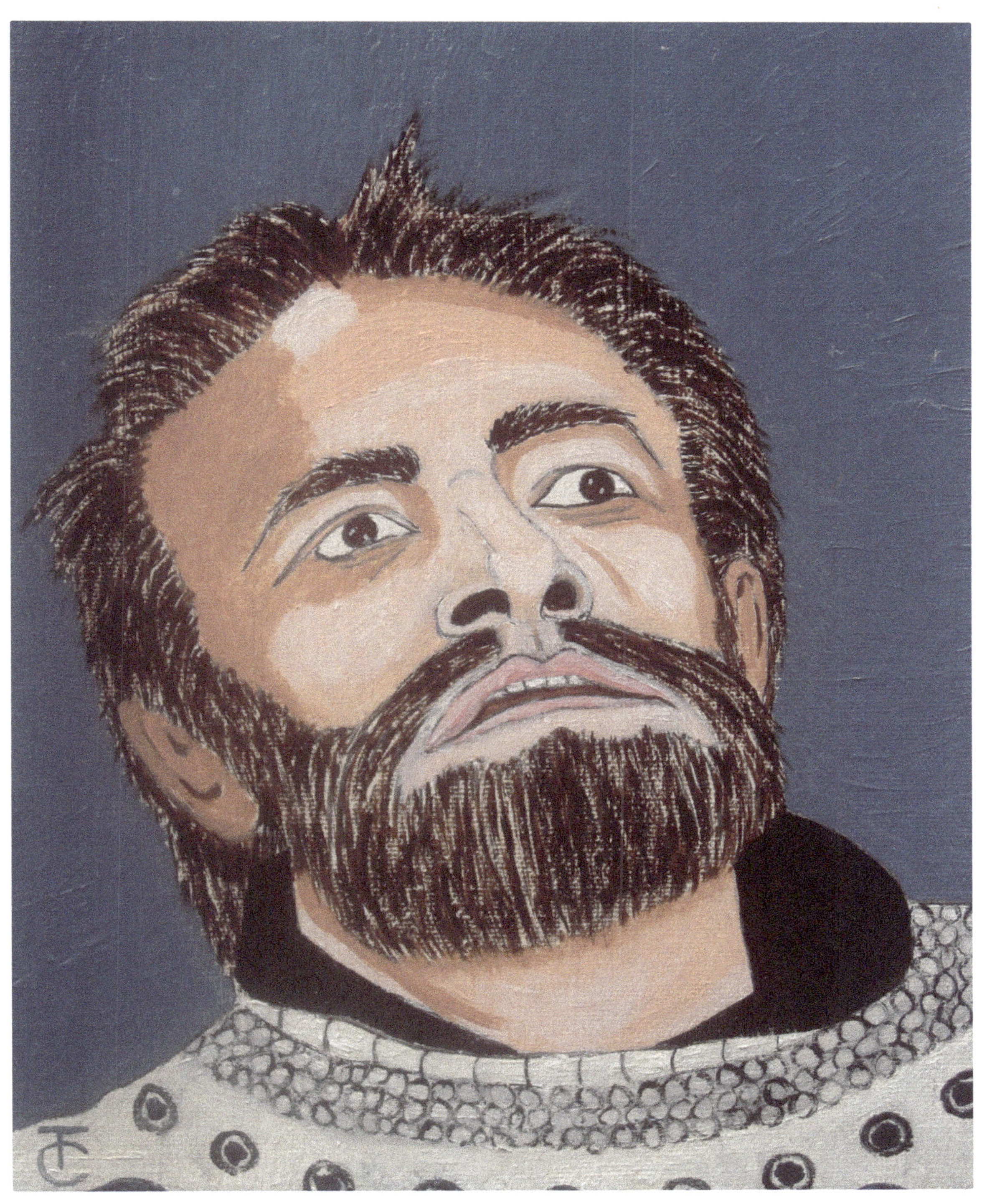

FRITZ WUNDERLICH
Tenor

Born in Kusel, Germany, in 1930; died in Heidelberg, Germany, 1966.
He joined the Frankfurt Opera in 1958 and moved to the Bavarian
State Opera in 1960. From 1962, he also appeared in Vienna.
His repertory included Don Ottavio, Alfredo, Lenski, Jenik
and Leukippos. He created Tiresias in Orff's *Oedipus* (1959)
and Christoph in Egk's *Verlobung* in *Santo Domingo* (1963).
He made his Covent Garden debut as Ottavio (*Don Giovanni*)
in 1965. He was scheduled to make his Met debut in
the same role but died after a fall in 1966.

Fritz Wunderlich as Valzacchi
(*Der Rosenkavalier*)

Der Rosenkavalier, opera in 3 acts by **Richard Strauss,**
first performed at the Royal Opera House, Dresden, January26, 1911.

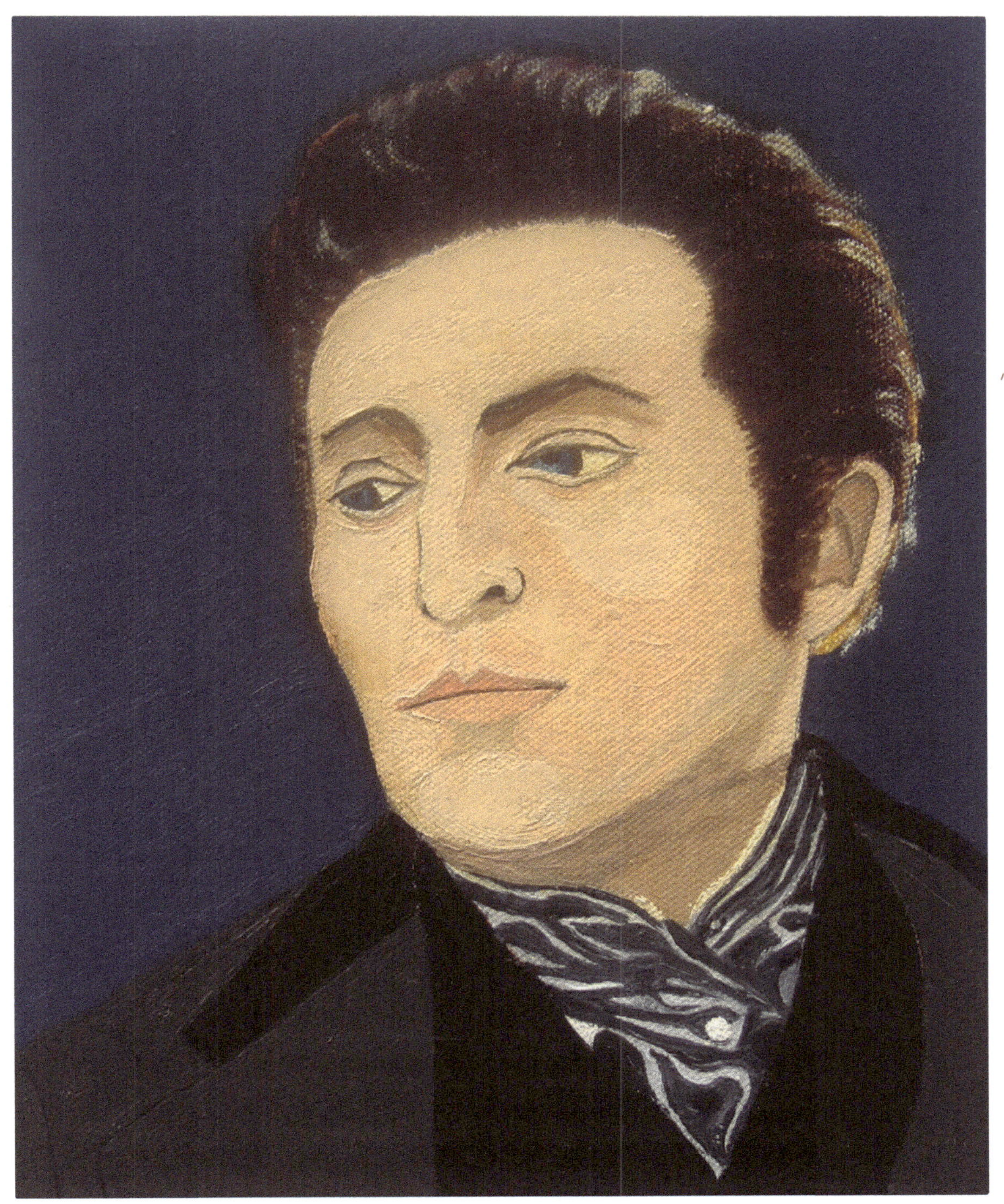

COMPOSERS

LUDWIG van BEETHOVEN, born in Bonn, Germany, 1770; died in Vienna, Austria, 1827. Beethoven's only opera, *Fidelio*, was composed during the composer's "heroic period" (1803-08) when his output was nearly superhuman. Beethoven revised *Fidelio* twice and the third version, which is regularly performed today, contains passages of sublime beauty and pure musical genius.

VINCENZO BELLINI, born in Catania, Sicily, 1801; died in Putreaux, France, 1835. The young composer achieved international fame with the premiere of his opera, *Il Pirata*, at La Scala in 1827. That success was followed by *La Straniera* (1829), *I Capuleti e I Montecchi* (1830), *La Sonnambula* (1831) and *Norma* (1831). Bellini moved from Milan to Paris in 1833 and became friends with Rossini, Chopin and other musicians. There he received a commission to compose *I Puritani di Scozia*, his last and greatest success, which opened at Paris's Theatre-Italien, in 1835.

HECTOR BERLIOZ, born in La Cote-St-André, Isere, France, 1803; died in Paris, France, 1869. Berlioz's first publicly performed opera was *Benvenuto Cellini* (1838). *La Damnation de Faust*, based on Goethe's *Faust*, was premiered in 1846; *Beatrice et Benedict*, a 2-act opera comique, opened in 1862; and *Les Troyens*, his masterpiece, in 1863.

GEORGES BIZET, born in Paris, France, 1838; died in Bougival, France, 1875. *Carmen*, premiered in 1874, the year before Bizet's death, is perhaps the most popular and widely performed opera ever composed. Other notable works by the composer are: *Don Procopio*, first performed posthumously in 1906, and *Les Pecheurs de Perles* (1863).

LEO DELIBES, born in St. Germain du Val, France, 1836; died in Paris, France, 1891. Delibes wrote more than 12 operettas, including the highly successful *Deux Vieilles Gardes* (1856), before his first attempt at a full-scale opera, *Le Roi l'a Dit* (1873). He composed two brilliant and enduring ballets, *Coppelia* (1870) and *Sylvia* (1876) before composing his masterpiece, *Lakmé* (1883).

GAETANO DONIZETTI, born in Bergamo, Italy, 1797; died in Bergamo, Italy, 1848. His facility, skill and versatility enabled Donizetti to produce many enduring works from farces to tragedies. His best works include: *Anna Bolena* (1830), *L'Elisir d'Amore* (1832), *Lucrezia Borgia* (1833), *Maria Stuarda* (1834), *Lucia di Lammermoor* (1835), *Roberto Devereux* (1837), *La Fille du Régiment* (1840), *La Favorite* (1840) and *Don Pasquale* (1842).

CHARLES FRANCIS GOUNOD, born in Paris, France, 1818; died in St.Cloud, France, 1893. Gounod's greatest success was *Faust,* composed from *Faust* by Goethe (1859). Other works include *Sappho* (1851), *Le Médecin malgre lui* (1858), and *Romeo et Juliette* (1867)

LEOS JANACEK, born in Hukvaldy, Moravia, 1854; died in Moravska, Ostrava, Czechoslavakia, 1928. His most successful operas are *Jenufa* (1904), *Katya Kabanova* (1921), *The Cunning Little Vixen* (1924), *The Makropoulos Affair* (1926), and *From the House of the Dead* (1930).

RUGGIERO LEONCAVALLO, born in Naples, Italy, 1857; died in Montecatini, Italy, 1919. Before composing his masterpiece, *I Pagliacci* (1892), Leoncavallo was an itinerant pianist and worked on the libretto of Puccini's *Manon Lescaut*. He composed two other operas that have had modest success and occasional revivals, *La Bohème* (1897) and *Zazà* (1900).

PIETRO MASCAGNI, born in Livorno, Italy, 1863; died in Rome, Italy, 1945. Mascagni's masterpiece, *Cavaleria Rusticana*, was such an immediate success that it had 60 curtain calls on the first night in 1890. The following year, his lyrical pastoral *L'Amico Fritz* was well received and has endured. His other operas are largely forgotten.

JULES MASSENET, born in Montand, France, 1842; died in Paris, France, 1912. His best operas include *Hérodiade* (1881), *Manon* (1884), *Esclarmonde* (1889), *Werther* (1892), *Thais* (1894) and *Griselidis* (1901).

GIACOMO MEYERBEER, born in Vogelsdorf, Germany, 1791; died in Paris, France, 1864. The composer's first German operas were unsuccessful. He went to Italy in 1915 and thereafter composed several acclaimed Italian operas: *Robert le Diable* (1831), *Les Huguenots* (1836), *Le Prophète* (1840), *L'Étoile du Nord* (1854) and *L'Africaine* (1864).

WOLFGANG AMADEUS MOZART, born in Salzburg, Austria, 1756; died in Vienna, Austria, 1791. Mozart's genius spanned the musical spectrum, of which opera was only a part, but many consider him the greatest opera composer, particularly for those works composed with the librettos of his collaborator, Lorenzo da Ponte: *Le Nozze di Figaro* (1786), *Don Giovanni* (1787) and *Cosi fan Tutte* (1790). Other works include *Idomeneo* (1781), *Die Entfuehrung aus dem Serail* (1782), *La Clemenza di Tito* (1791) and *Die Zauberfloete* (1791).

MODEST MOUSSORGSKY, born in Karevo, Russia, 1839; died in St. Petersburg, Russia, 1881. *Boris Godunov*, a masterpiece of Russian music, is the only opera that Moussorgsky completed. It was first perfomed in both London and at the Met in 1913. *Sorocinskaja Jarmarka* was first publicly performed in Moscow in 1913. *Khovanshcina*, completed and orchestrated by Rimsky-Korsakov was first peformed in St. Petersburg in 1886.

JACQUES OFFENBACH, born in Cologne, Germany, 1819; died
in Paris, France, 1880. The composer's masterpiece, *Les Contes
d'Hoffmann*, was unfinished at his death and completed posthumously
in 1881. Other works include: *Orphee aux Enfers* (1858), *La Belle Hélène*
(1864), *La Vie Parisienne* (1866), *La Grande Duchesse de Gerolstein*
(1867) and *La Perichole* (1868).

GIACOMO PUCCINI, born in Lucca, Italy, 1858; died in Brussels,
Belguim, 1924. The master of *opera verismo*, Puccini composed three
of the most popular operas in history, *La Bohème* (1896), *Tosca* (1900),
and *Madama Butterfly* (1904). Other significant works include
Manon Lescaut (1893), *La Fanciulla del West* (1910),
Gianni Schicchi (1918), and *Turandot* (1926).

GIOACCHINO ROSSINI, born in Pesaro, Italy, 1792; died in Passy,
France, 1868. The composer's most performed works include *Tancredi*
(1813), *L'Italiana in Algeri* (1813), *Il Turco in Italia* (1814), *Il Barbiere
di Siviglia* (1816), *La Cenerentola* (1817), *La Donna del Lago* (1819),
Semiramide (1823), *Le Siège de Corinthe* (1826),
Le Comte Ory (1828), and *Guillaume Tell* (1829).

BEDRICH SMETANA, born in Litomysl, Bohemia in 1824; died in Prague, Czechoslavakia, 1884. *The Bartered Bride*, the first of Smetana's operas, was conducted by the composer at its premiere in 1866. His revision, completed and performed in 1870, is undoubtedly his operatic masterpiece. Other works are: *Dalibor* (1868), *The Kiss* (1876), *The Secret* (1878) and *Libuse* (1881).

RICHARD STRAUSS, born in Munich, Germany, 1864; died in Garmisch-Partinkirchen, Bavaria, 1949. Strauss's first operatic success, *Salome* (1905) was an international success and something of a scandal because of Salome's "Dance of the Seven Veils." Strauss's relatively early success was followed by a diverse series of enduring operas: *Electra* (1909), *Der Rosenkavalier* (1911), *Ariadne auf Naxos* (1912), *Die Frau ohne Schatten* (1919), *Arabella* (1933) and *Capriccio* (1942).

GIUSEPPE VERDI, born in Roncole, Italy, 1813; died in Milan, Italy, 1901. Generally considered the greatest Italian opera composer, his finest works include *Nabucco* (1842), *Macbeth* (1847), *Luisa Miller* (1849), *Rigoletto* (1851), *Il Trovatore* (1853), *La traviata* (1853), *Simon Boccanegra* (1857), *Un ballo in maschera* (1859), *La forza del destino* (1862), *Don Carlos* (1867), *Aida* (1871), *Otello* (1887) and *Falstaff* (1893).

RICHARD WAGNER, born in Leipzig, Germany, 1813; died in Venice, Italy, 1883. The most successful operas composed by the greatest German opera composer include: *Der fliegende Hollaender* (1843), *Tannhaeuser* (1845), *Lohengrin* (1850), *Tristan und Isolde* (1865), *Die Meistersinger von Nuernberg* (1868), and the ring cycle: *Das Rheingold* (1869), *Die Walkuere* (1870), *Siegfried* (1876), *Goetterdaemmerung* (1876), and *Parsifal* (1882).